About this book...

This book is a must read for anyone involved in creating a product; management, testers and developers. Use it to change the way you think projects should be run and close those communication gaps.

— Toby Henderson

Have you ever wanted a better way to communicate, clarify and satisfy business requirements? Wouldn't it be great if those requirements evolved along with the software, always consistent and clear? And those requirements helped drive development so that we knew when we were done? With clarity, Gojko describes an elegance and effective way of achieving this with the whole team: Inventing, thinking and communicating with specific, insightful examples that also serve as acceptance tests.

— Rick Mugridge, www.rimuresearch.com, and lead author of 'Fit for Developing Software', Prentice Hall, 2005.

Effective software development is all about good communication and this book explains the toolkit that allows us to do this effectively. Worth reading whatever your role is.

— Mark Needham, http://www.markhneedham.com/blog/

Whether you're new to testing, new to agile, or an old pro at one or both, you'll experience "aha" moments that will inspire your team as you read. This book will challenge some of your preconceived notions and make you think. It paves the way for people in different roles, such as business analysts, QA engineers and developers, to adapt to a more productive agile approach. From practical ways to improve communication with customers, to helpful examples of useful test tools, this book is a major addition to our agile testing knowledge base.

— Lisa Crispin, co-author, 'Agile Testing: A Practical Guide for Testers and Agile Teams', Addison-Wesley Professional 2009

Gojko addresses an underrated point: that Test-Driven Requirements, or Executable Requirements, are not about tools, automated tests, or even professionalism. They are about communication. I wish each of my colleagues and clients had a copy of his book, and maybe that fact will be made just a little bit clearer to them.

— Eric Lefevre-Ardant, Agile Coach and Developer, http://ericlefevre.net/

I wish that the book had been available a few years ago when the company I was at (and myself) were trying out agile. Could have been a lot easier and more successful if we'd read it.

— Philip Kirkham

If you've tried agile acceptance testing you'll know that as well as being really exciting it's also incredibly difficult. Luckily we now have a book that helps guide us through the many tricky choices that we face, practical and pragmatic advice that even the most experienced agile developer should be aware of.

— Colin Jack, Senior Software Developer, FNZ

As a tester, I welcome any opportunity to increase shared understanding of requirements and expectations - our team will be relying on this book to guide us as we begin our journey with agile acceptance testing.

— Marisa Seal

You would be at least 6 moths ahead of the game in Agile QA by just reading Gojko's book.

— Gennady Kaganer, QA Manager at Standard and Poor's

Gojko applies his experience to the practice of producing software that is useful to end users. This is an important work in extending the test-driven specification of software beyond individual units and into the sum of the parts.

— Bob Clancy, http://www.agiletester.net

Bridging the Communication Gap will not only bring you up-to-date with the latest thinking about agile acceptance testing, but also guide you as you put the ideas into practice. This book is packed with insights from Adzic's experience in the field.

— David Peterson, creator of the Concordion acceptance-testing framework

I'm convinced that the practice of agile acceptance testing, done properly, can make a dramatic improvement to both the communication with the customer and the quality of the final product. This book is a solid introduction to the subject, and represents the first attempt I've seen to survey the practice as a whole without focusing on a single tool or technology.

— Geoff Bache

Bridging the Communication Gap

Specification by Example and Agile Acceptance Testing

Gojko Adzic

Bridging the Communication Gap: Specification by Example and Agile Acceptance Testing

Gojko Adzic
Copy-editor: Marjory Bisset
Cover design: Boris Marcetic

Published 5 Jan 2009
Copyright © 2009 Neuri Limited

Neuri Limited
25 Southampton Buildings
London WC2A 1AL
United Kingdom

You can also contact us by e-mail: contact@neuri.com

Register your book online

Visit http://www.acceptancetesting.info and register your book online to get free PDF updates and notifications about corrections or future editions of this book.

ISBN: 978-0-9556836-1-9

Table of Contents

About the PDF edition

If you are reading this book in a print edition, you should know that there is a PDF version available, and you might find it useful to get an electronic copy as well. I've decided to make this book available as a PDF so that the readers can get the most out of it. Judging from the sales of my previous book, many people today prefer reading technical texts in an electronic form so that they can search through the content, copy and paste text and archive the material more easily.

If you are reading this as a PDF, please note that this material is copyrighted and it is not for free distribution. I have no intention of chasing people for redistributing the book, but if you have received this PDF from someone and you found it useful, consider actually purchasing your own copy. The PDF edition is relatively cheap and your purchase will support similar efforts in the future.

Buying a PDF or a printed version entitles you to free PDF updates. Register your copy and you'll receive a free PDF when the book is updated in the future. For more information on the PDF version of this book, and to register your copy, see:

http://www.acceptancetesting.info

Acknowledgements

This book is a result of a small independent publishing effort, and as such would not be possible without the help of many people.

I'd like to thank Antony Marcano, Bob Clancy, Colin Jack, David Peterson, David Vydra, Eric Lefevre-Ardant, Gennady Kaganer, Geoff Bache, Jennitta Andrea, Lisa Crispin, Marisa Seal, Mark Needham, Melissa Tan, Mike Scott, Phil Kirkham and Rick Mugridge for all the excellent suggestions, helping me keep this book focused and providing insight into their views and experiences. Without you, this book just would not be possible.

Marjory Bisset from Pearl Words again did a great job of copy-editing this book and ensuring that readers have a much more enjoyable experience with it.

Finally, I'd like to thank Boris Marcetic from Popular for designing the covers.

About the author

Gojko Adzic runs Neuri Ltd, a UK-based consultancy that helps companies build better software by introducing agile practices and tools and improving communication between software teams, stakeholders and clients. His programming story so far includes equity and energy trading, mobile positioning, e-commerce, betting and gaming and complex configuration management.

Gojko is the author of several popular printed and online guides on acceptance testing, including *Test Driven .NET Development with Fitnesse* and *Getting Fit with .NET*, and more than 200 articles about programming, operating systems, the Internet and new technologies published in various online and print magazines. He is the primary contributor to the DbFIT database testing library which is used by banks, insurance companies and bookmakers worldwide.

To get in touch, write to gojko@neuri.com or visit http://gojko.net.

Introduction

I am getting more and more convinced every day that communication is, in fact, what makes or breaks software projects. Programming tools, practices and methods are definitely important, but if the communication fails then the rest is just painting the corpse. Complex projects simply have no chance of success without effective communication.

This is a book about improving communication between customers, business analysts, developers and testers on software projects, especially by using specification by example and agile acceptance testing. Although these two practices are not yet popular, I consider them as key emerging software development practices because they can significantly improve the chances of success of a software project. (At the same time, agile acceptance testing is one of the worst named practices ever. For the time being, just forget that it has the word testing in the name.) Agile acceptance testing and specification by example essentially help us to close the communication gap between different participants in a software project, ensure that they speak the same language and build a truly shared and consistent understanding of the domain. This leads to better specifications – the participants flush out incorrect assumptions and discover functional gaps before the development starts and build software that is genuinely fit for purpose.

Ward Cunningham and Ken Auer used the basic ideas behind agile acceptance testing to nail down what their users wanted in 1999.[1] Almost a decade later, the practice is still used only by a small group of early adopters. However, it has matured considerably. Judging from recent conferences, magazine articles and blog posts, it seems to me that interest is growing and the time is right for a wider group to learn about and adopt it. You probably agree, which is why you picked up this book.

---

[1] See *Don't just break software, make software*[1]

Why should you care?

Agile acceptance testing and specification by example help business people, software developers and testers communicate better and understand each other. Each of these groups has different needs and problems in a software project, so improved communication has different benefits for them. In this section, I briefly list the the benefits agile acceptance testing and specification by example will deliver for each group. The rest of this book explains how to achieve these benefits.

These are the most important benefits for product owners, business analysts and project managers:

- Developers will actually read the specifications that you write.
- You will be sure that developers and testers understand the specifications correctly.
- You will be sure that they do not skip parts of the specifications.
- You can track development progress easily.
- You can easily identify conflicts in business rules and requirements caused by later change requests.
- You'll save time on acceptance and smoke testing.

From a developer's perspective, these are the most important advantages of agile acceptance testing and specification by example:

- Most functional gaps and inconsistencies in the requirements and specifications will be flushed out before the development starts.
- You will be sure that business analysts actually understand special cases that you want to discuss with them.
- You will have automated tests as targets to help you focus the development.
- It will be easier to share, hand over and take over code.

From a tester's perspective, these are the most important benefits of agile acceptance testing and specification by example:

- You can influence the development process and stop developers from making the same mistakes over and over.
- You will have a much better understanding of the domain.
- You'll delegate a lot of dull work to developers, who will collaborate with you on automating the verifications.
- You can build in quality from the start by raising concerns about possible problems before the development starts.
- You'll be able to verify business rules with a touch of a button.
- You will have a lot more time for exploratory testing.
- You will be able to build better relationships with developers and business people and get their respect.

Who is this book for?

This book is primarily intended for product owners, business analysts, software developers and testers who want to learn about how to implement agile acceptance testing and how to improve communication on their projects. It should also prove to be interesting to project managers working on agile software projects or in the process of migrating to an agile methodology. I wrote this book both for people working in implementation teams and for people working on the customer side, and for teams that practice agile development as well as those who are migrating to an agile process. I use the term *implementation team* in this book as a name for the entire group of people working on a project, from business analysts to developers, testers and anyone else involved.

Although agile teams generally strive for less role-naming than those practising traditional processes, I use the role names *product owner*, *business analyst, software developer* and *tester* in this book and discuss how each of these roles is affected by agile acceptance testing and how they participate in writing specifications by example. Companies in transition with teams coming from a more traditional background will have all these roles clearly defined, sometimes isolated into different departments, buildings or even countries. Most agile programming literature is written by software developers for software developers, leaving testers and business analysts to fend for themselves and try to work out what they should be doing. Agile acceptance testing requires active participation from all project implementation team members, including business analysts and testers, not just developers. This is why I want to use these roles and names to emphasise their involvement in the process. Contrary to common belief, it is not unusual for larger agile projects to have dedicated business analysts and testers. ThoughtWorks is generally accepted as one of the leading agile software development companies and their process has these roles clearly defined and uses these names.[2]

The roles of business analysts and testers on agile projects differ somewhat from their roles on projects that use more traditional formal methods, but this does not mean that the people behind these roles do not exist. Roles are blurred a bit, but specialists still have to focus on particular areas. If you are a business analyst or a tester, this book should help you define more accurately what your job is and how to make a more useful contribution to building software the agile way.

What will you get out of this book?

Primarily, this book will help you to get started and implement agile acceptance testing and specification by example effectively. It explains the principles and ideas behind the practice and helps you put it into the wider context of your development process.

As with any other new and relatively radical idea, learning how to apply it effectively in your own role is only part of the challenge. Agile acceptance testing requires active participation and affects the jobs of programmers, business analysts, testers and to some extent project managers. Because of this, it also raises a lot of concerns and it is unfortunately subject to many misconceptions. These problems are typically fuelled by partial information, misunderstandings and fears of change. One of my primary goals with this book is to dispel these

---

[2]http://download.microsoft.com/documents/uk/msdn/architecture/architectinsight/2007/Life-cycle/LIF02-The-Agile-Template-for-VSTS.ppt.

misconceptions and address fears and issues that people often have about agile acceptance testing.

It is also my intention with this book to challenge some established ways of thinking in the industry. Agile acceptance testing breaks down traditional boundaries around testing, requirements and specification processes in a way that significantly improves communication on a project. Specification by example is an approach to the writing of specifications and requirements radically different from the established industry process. I will explain this in a lot more detail throughout the book, but please note that if you come from a more traditional software process background, you may need to put aside the stereotypes that you are familiar with in order to grasp the ideas and gain the full benefits.

This book will help you to discover how agile acceptance testing affects your work whether you are a programmer, business analyst or a tester. It will help you gain an understanding of this technique and offer ideas on how to convince other team members and stakeholders to use it. I hope that this book takes into account the various perspectives of these different roles. It is intentionally not too technical or suited only for programmers, because agile acceptance testing is not a programming technique: it is a communication technique that brings people involved in a software project closer. I consider myself primarily a programmer and my personal biases and experiences will surely show. I have, however, found a much broader perspective on agile acceptance testing as a result of working with different teams, consulting, mentoring and giving public talks. Discussing fears such as losing jobs with testers over coffee, participating in requirements gathering, working as a product owner and even as a business domain expert on several projects has hopefully given me the understanding necessary to represent the needs and views of the other roles.

What's inside?

I am very proud of the fact that I have helped several companies adopt agile acceptance testing and specification by example and deliver successful software over the last few years. This book is a summary of my experiences, learnings and ideas from this journey. It is based on projects that are now happily running in production and a series of public and private seminars, talks and workshops that I organised during this period.

This book contains a description of the process that I use today to bridge the communication gap between business people and software implementation teams. More importantly, it describes ideas, principles and practices behind the process and their effects on people participating in software projects.

This book is not a detailed user manual for any acceptance testing tool. Although I will describe briefly some of the most popular tools in Chapter 10, I intentionally want to keep this book relatively non-technical and absolutely not tool or technology specific. Often I hear from managers that their teams looked into this or that tool and that they did not like it a bit, so they rejected the whole idea of agile acceptance testing. One of the main messages I want to convey with this book is that the biggest benefit of agile acceptance testing is improved communication and mutual understanding, not test automation. There is too much focus on tools today and in my opinion this is quite wrong.

While you are reading this book, it's important to focus on the ideas and principles. The process and the tools described in the book are there just to assist. If you do not like a particular tool, find a better one or automate things yourself in a way that makes sense for your team. If you do not like some part of the process, adjust it or replace it with something that makes more sense for your team. Once you understand the underlying ideas, principles and practices, applying them in your environment should be easy. Use the process described in this book just as a guide, not as a prescription.

This book also does not have all the answers about agile acceptance testing and specification by example. These two practices are currently gaining a lot of momentum and generating a lot of new ideas. Because there is very little published material on them at the moment, you will see many more references to conference talks, blog posts and online video clips than to books or articles. Apart from the practices as I use them today, this book also describes some promising ideas that I want to try out in the near future. It even contains some interesting views of other people that I do not agree with completely. Some of them might prove to be interesting in the future with better tools or be applicable in a different environment. In Chapter 11 I speculate how the tools for agile acceptance testing tools might evolve. Blogs, mailing lists and sites listed in Appendix A will help you continue the journey and keep up-to-date with new advances.

Giving credit where credit is due

I make no claim and take no credit for inventing any of the ideas or techniques that are described in this book. The techniques I describe are based on ideas I have picked up on the way from books, conferences, blogs, discussion groups and colleagues. This book is an attempt to collect different techniques that have emerged in the community, show how they relate to each other and organise them in a one coherent practice.

Agile acceptance testing is an evolution of the idea of *customer tests* proposed by Kent Beck in which automated tests are used to verify what the customers expect out of a software system. It also draws on ideas developed by many others. Gerald Weinberg and Donald Gause used the *black-box requirements testing* process to redefine the role of tests in a project and relate them directly to requirements. Brian Marick has done great work on bringing tests closer to the business by clearly defining *business-facing tests.* He is also one of the key promoters of the idea of *specification by example,* where realistic examples are used instead of abstract requirements. Dan North's ideas of *behaviour-driven development* bring acceptance testing closer to business people. Ron Jeffries described the *card-conversation-confirmation* concept nailing down the basic ideas behind specification workshops and linking acceptance tests to user stories. Joshua Kerievsky's *storytest-driven development* expands on this to fit acceptance testing into agile planning techniques. Jim Shore defined the *describe-demonstrate-develop* process as a way to use acceptance tests iteratively to focus development. Lisa Crispin and Antony Marcano were instrumental to promoting and improving *agile testing* practices, tearing down the walls between testers and developers and business people. Eric Evans came up with the idea of *ubiquitous language*, used to avoid confusion caused by different jargons on a project.

These ideas are supplemented by the practices and knowledge embodied in Ward Cunningham's tool FIT and Object Mentor's tool FitNesse, along with many other similar tools and extension libraries, especially Rick Mugridge's FitLibrary and the learning that came out of using these tools in commercial projects. David Peterson's focus on *specifications over scripting* with Concordion is instrumental to getting the most out of agile acceptance testing. A lot of the underlying principles come from *test-driven development*, which in turn borrows a lot of ideas from the *zero quality control* idea of Shigeo Shingo and the *Toyota Production System* of Taichi Ono along with their counterparts in the software world, the *lean software development* ideas of Mary and Tom Poppendieck. Effective application of agile acceptance testing depends on various practices such as short iterations from Scrum, Extreme Programming and other agile processes and the work on *user stories* by Mike Cohn and others. Some ideas are even borrowed from Prussian military tactics from the nineteenth century and their current implementation in the US Army.

Agile acceptance testing is more than the sum of all these ideas and practices. It is an approach to software development characterised by a focus on communication and the creation of an understanding of the domain shared by all implementation team members and customers.

How this book is organised

In Part I, I present causes of the communication problems in software projects, explain why the traditional model of building requirements and specifications does not work and how other agile programming practices do not really solve the problem but only provide work-arounds. Then I introduce agile acceptance testing as the solution to these problems.

In Part II, I introduce the techniques and principles of agile acceptance testing and explain how they work together to help us facilitate communication and build better software.

In Part III, I talk about implementing agile acceptance testing in organisations. I explain how this practice fits into the wider software development process and how to start using it in your organisation. I also briefly describe current popular tools for agile acceptance testing and discuss what can we expect from future tools. This part also includes a chapter on user stories, another agile technique that makes the implementation of agile acceptance testing much easier.

In Part IV, I deal with the human side of this practice, explaining how it affects our jobs and the way we work. I analyse the effects on business analysts, testers and developers. The chapter on the effects on business analysts is also applicable to customers or other business people involved in software projects. In this part we also revisit the benefits listed in section *Why should you care?* on page xvi and see how the principles and practices described this book deliver them.

Part I. The Communication Gap

Effective communication is the key to successful software projects. In this part, we set the stage by looking at common communication problems on software projects, analysing what happens when communication is impeded and how we can improve the flow of information.

Chapter 1
The next bottleneck in software projects

The world of software development went through quite a shake-up in the last decade. Extreme programming and other early agile development practices removed several huge bottlenecks in the way we were used to working, allowing software teams to deliver faster, better and react to changes more easily. Once these problems were out of the way, people started noticing other issues in projects such as planning and organisation. Looking for a better way to manage projects, agile development teams adopted the Scrum methodology. A whole range of related techniques emerged to remove planning and organisational bottlenecks. Agile development and management practices are now mature and widely accepted and I feel confident that the technical part of building software is no longer a problem. The most important issue now is making sure that we know what we need to build, but this problem is a whole lot harder than it sounds.

Of course, this problem is nothing new. Fred Brooks wrote long ago that "The hardest single part of building a software system is deciding precisely what to build"[2]. Practices used in the creation of traditional system requirements documents and specifications have changed very little over the last decade. Some techniques such as user stories touch upon what we should do to get better specifications and requirements, but they fall short of completing the task to the end. The process of eliciting requirements and communicating them throughout the process to everyone involved is often just described in vague terms and left to teams to work out for themselves. With programming practices and project planning now pretty well sorted, this issue is becoming more and more apparent and many teams realise that they struggle with it. This problem is the next bottleneck to be removed from the software development process.

A nice thing about software development the agile way is that we can easily go back and adjust the system, but making changes is not as cheap as most programmers would like it to be. It costs a lot of money and time. For those of you who would now suggest that using agile practices makes this cheap, don't forget that you are only talking about the technical cost. Agile practices help us cope with clients changing their minds for whatever reason, so that in a sense we are hitting a moving target. There is a huge difference between this and missing a still target and then going back to have another go at hitting it. Even if the requirements don't change, there is still a risk that the project can miss a target if we don't solve the communication problems. Although agile practices help a lot with reducing the risk of failure, they should not and cannot be used to cover up for a project that simply does not deliver what it was supposed to. Disappointing a client is never good, agile or not agile. Gerald Weinberg and Donald Gause suggest that the difference between disappointment and delight is not a matter of delivering software, but how well the delivery matches what clients expected.[1] This was true twenty years ago when they wrote *Exploring Requirements*[3], and it still holds true today.

Matching what clients expect is still a problem, mostly because of communication issues. Individual effects of small communication problems are very hard to detect, so they do not become apparent instantly. Such problems are reflected in lots of small things not working as expected or implied features that simply do not get delivered. Individual issues may have small effects on the project, but their cumulative effect is huge. The reason why changes in development practices in the last ten years have not solved this problem is that most of these changes were driven by developers and I do not believe that this particular issue is a development problem at all. It is a communication problem involving all participants in the implementation team. This is why there is no development practice that can solve the problem, whether or not it demands the involvement of customer proxies and business people.

---

[1] See chapter 18 of Exploring Requirements[3]

We all need to agree on what the target is, even if it moves, and make sure that we all have the same understanding. And by *we* I mean all participants in the process from stakeholders to domain experts, business analysts, testers and developers. The path to success is to ensure that these small communication problems get rooted out instead of accumulating, so that the message gets delivered correctly and completely.

The telephone game

The traditional model of gathering requirements and building specifications is based on a lot of formalising, handing over and translating. Business analysts first extract knowledge about requirements from customers, formalising it into specifications and handing it over to developers and testers. Developers extract knowledge from this and translate it into executable code, which is handed over to testers. Testers then take the specifications, extract knowledge from them and translate it into verification scripts, which are then applied to the code that was handed over to them by the developers.

In theory, this works just fine and everyone is happy. In practice, this process is essentially flawed and the usual result is a huge difference between what was originally requested and what gets actually delivered. There can be huge communication gaps at every step. Important ideas fall through these gaps and mysteriously disappear. After every translation, information gets distorted and misunderstood, magnifying the degree of wrongness of the delivered system. A tester's independent interpretation might help to correct the false interpretations of developers, or it might very well be a completely different misinterpretation of the system requirements.

With agile development processes, the feedback loop is much shorter then in a traditional process, so problems get discovered quickly. However, if agile acceptance testing is not applied, even with other agile practices in place, there is still a lot of scope for mistakes. Instead of discovering problems, we need to work out how to stop them from appearing in the first place.

People seem somehow surprised by this effect even though most of us have encountered it and used to amusing effects in childhood. Antony Marcano draws a parallel between the traditional software development process and the *telephone game*.[2] In the telephone game (called Chinese whispers in the UK) a group of children stand in line and then the first child whispers a phrase or sentence to the next child. The second child whispers what it heard to the third one and so on. The last child in the line says aloud the phrase or sentence that it heard. It is often significantly different from the original phrase. Although these cumulative differences may have been amusing when we were children; they are not so funny when it comes to solving real problems that obstruct people in doing their jobs. What happens with the traditional approach is that quite a few things get lost in translation. Even when people do read big documents carefully, they don't remember all the details. Most people just digest the text looking for key ideas and guidelines, disregarding everything else.

Relying on people to remember all the details is futile. This is why features rarely get implemented completely and correctly at the first attempt, so that the project relies on testers running through the specification documents and comparing them with what has been developed. This again poses a challenge since testers often get involved only when the party is over and they are expected to understand instantly a complex software system without taking too much of the 'precious' developers' time on explaining things. As tight deadlines are a rule rather than an exception these days, testers don't have a lot of time to learn about the development and system specifications. They are often expected to approve a release in just a few days. This makes it hard for them to really understand what they are testing and severely undermines the effectiveness of testing.

Although big specification documents give the impression of consti-tuting complete and comprehensive descriptions of requirements, in practice (at least the ones I have seen) they often leave out some details that need to be worked out later via e-mail or in a whole series of other documents. The original specification is, in such cases, out of date as

---

[2]http://www.testingreflections.com/node/view/7232

soon as the development starts. Even with perfectly correct, complete and detailed specifications, there is still a possibility that requirements will change during development. This is a rule rather than an exception for longer projects. Changes get implemented directly without updating specifications, leading to differences between code and system documentation. In this case the specifications are technically incorrect. So if the testers identify a difference between the system and the original documents, this does not necessarily mean that they found a problem. This makes the job of testers even harder, because they cannot rely completely on the specifications.

Such differences between what was asked for and what was developed may also come from unclear or inconsistent requirements. Code is unforgiving with regards to specifying how something should work. On this level, we have to define exactly how the system should behave. Once developers start writing code, gaps in functionality become obvious. Unfortunately, getting to domain experts or business people who wrote the specifications at this point may take a while. In the best case, developers need to get the person on the phone or chase her by e-mail. If the person in charge is an external customer or an executive project sponsor, they might not be readily available to talk and it might take a few days to get the right information. In some extreme cases, it is nearly impossible. During a workshop I organised for a large media company, one of the developers said that their business analysts actually refuse to discuss requirements after they were handed over to development. According to their process, the job of business analysts was done at that point.

Because developers need to specify how the system works in the newly identified case and they need to seek out this information, the time to complete a piece of code increases from several minutes to several hours or several days. When the gaps are finally cleared up, the original specification document again may not reflect the full reality. There is at least some new functionality not covered by the document, or it may even conflict with the original requirements.

Later on, when requests for changes and improvements start coming in, especially if the product has several clients with different requirements, changes may break earlier rules or introduce inconsistencies into the system. Depending on regression test coverage, this problem might surface or be noticed only in production.

The problem is, of course, that not even the brightest among us can keep track of all the previous requirements and all the changes in their minds for a long period of time. Realistically, it's not sane to expect someone to remember all 500 pages of a specification document and instantly spot that a new change request might break an earlier rule. This becomes even harder when the people involved in the original project move on to other things and are replaced. With big requirements documents, consistency can be a problem even in the initial phase, since they might be the result of several days of discussions with different people, and are sometimes written by several people.

Imperative requirements are very easy to misunderstand

With agile development processes, it is less likely that business analysts will produce great long documents that caused a small forest to be cut down. Requirements are typically broken down and iteratively constructed and communicated. This does not really make a huge difference with regards to the communication problems that I want to attack. Without agile acceptance testing, agile processes will potentially help us catch a problem sooner because on-site customers provide feedback, but they do not prevent the problem from happening. Requirements are simply subject to interpretation and quite often to misinterpretation. Imperative requirements, which command what people should do without demonstrating it, are especially bad as they are seemingly precise but leave quite a lot of potential for mistakes. We each have our own assumptions that affect the way we understand these statements. The fact that we have heard, read and understood something in English does not necessarily mean that we understood it in the same way.

The story about a series of experiments conducted by Lawrence G. Shattuck with four active battalions of the US Army,[3] quoted in Gary Klein's book *Sources of Power*[4], illustrates this problem nicely. The researchers attended a military exercise and listened in while the commanders were giving orders to their teams. During the exercise, they wrote down everything that the teams did. After the exercise, they discussed the actual actions of the teams with the commanders. The results of the research were that actions on the ground matched commanders' expectations completely only in 34% of the cases. While I was reading it, it struck me how this story completely relates to my early experiences in software development. The commanders are customers or business analysts, the orders are requirements or specifications and the teams on the ground are developers and testers. We all sit in the same room, listen to the customers, agree on the requirements and specifications and then go away and develop something that often does not match completely what the customers want. I don't know of any similar experiments actually being conducted with software development teams, but I would not imagine that the result is a lot different. In a sense, the story about the same thing happening in the US Army is comforting because it means that we are not the only ones plagued by misunderstandings and wrong assumptions. Unfortunately, this comforting feeling quickly goes away if you think about the fact that these guys have the biggest guns in the world and that they misunderstand orders twice in every three times.

Are obvious things really obvious?

A very serious problem with requirements is taking obvious things for granted. In Exploring Requirements[3], Gause and Weinberg described an experiment from one of their workshops that shows how even the simplest things can be misinterpreted. They showed a seven-pointed star picture to attendees before a seminar, then held a lecture and let people have a coffee break. After the break, they asked the attendees to tell them how many points the picture had. They received

---

[3]http://www.au.af.mil/au/awc/awcgate/milreview/shattuck.pdf

quite a wide spread of results. According to Gause and Weinberg, everyone knows what a five-pointed star looks like but their star was more unusual, so people remembered it differently and recalled different images, especially after the coffee break. This accounted for the spread. People also understood the task differently, which explained clusters in the answers.

In August 2008, I repeated this experiment,[4] focusing only on differences in interpretation. During a talk, I handed out index cards, put a picture of a standard five-pointed star on the projector and asked the attendees to write down how many points they saw in the picture. I used an image of a familiar figure (Figure 1.1) and it was on display while people wrote down their answers, so that observation and memory problems would not affect the answers. Any differences in answers could only be caused by people interpreting the task differently. After some initial reluctance and explaining that the question might sound stupid and obvious, but people should answer it anyway, I got more than 40 cards back.

An interesting thing about this experiment is that most people are absolutely certain that there is an obvious answer, because the question seems so simple. The real problem is that although people have an obvious single logical answer in their heads ('the only possible answer'), this answer differs from person to person (Figure 1.2). Twenty five people voted for ten points in the star, counting inner and outer points. The second most popular answer with seven votes was five points, where people counted just the outer points. Six people voted for fourteen – one of the attendees explained that this is probably the ten points on the star and the four corners of the picture. Note that there was no border on the picture, but some people decided to count the edges of the screen as well. There was a single vote for nine points, which can theoretically be explained by five outer points and four corners of the picture. A reader of my blog later suggested that eleven would be a natural answer for someone with a vector graphics background, who would consider that the end point and starting point are different points even though they are physically in

---

[4]http://gojko.net/2008/08/29/how-many-points-are-there-in-a-five-point-star/

the same place. The two votes for fifteen are still a mystery to me. Bob Clancy suggested that this might be a classic example of the original problem being restated by the individual and than the restated problem solved: if the star is drawn with lines crossing in the inside of the star and then a point counted wherever two lines intersect, people might count the points in the inner pentagon twice (although they are the same as the five inner points).

Figure 1.1. A standard five-pointed star... but how many points does it have?

Some readers are now probably asking themselves what is the right answer. In general, there is no right answer. Or more precisely, all of these answers are correct, depending on what you consider a point. *In software projects, on the other hand, there is a single correct answer in similar situations: the one that the business people thought of.* And for the project to turn out just the way that customers want, this answer has to come up in the heads of developers and testers as well. This is quite a lot of mental alignment. Forty cards are not a sample large enough for statistical relevance, but this experiment has confirmed that even a simple thing such as a familiar image and a straightforward question can be interpreted in many different ways.

Figure 1.2. Results of my poll on points in the star

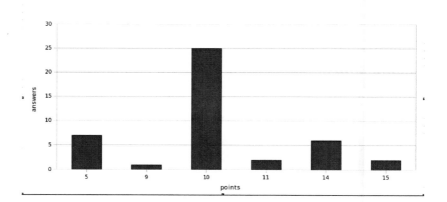

Imagine that you are part of a software project that calculates prices for gold-plating various metal pieces. This may be a contrived example, but let's keep it simple for now. One of the requirements, in its classical imperative form, states that "the system shall let the users enter a diameter and the number of points of a star-shaped metal piece and calculate the price of gold-plating based on materials (total piece surface area using prices in appendix A) and complexity (number of edges using prices in appendix B)". We have the prices and formulas precisely defined in imaginary appendices and the business analyst has spent a lot of time getting these absolutely clear with the customers, because this is where the money is. Developers should be able to work out the rest easily from the number of points in the star and the diameter and testers should be able to compare the test results to expected results easily. After all, everything is specified precisely and we only have to do a bit of elementary geometry. Right? Well, not exactly.

When requirements finally come to development, things become much more precise because someone actually has to write the code. Bertrand Russell wrote in *The Philosophy of Logical Atomism*[5] that "Everything is vague to a degree you do not realise till you have tried to make it precise". On most projects even today, writing code is the first time that we try to make the solution really precise. At this point, a developer may have the same understanding of a point as the business person making the request, but I would not bet on it. Work out the probabilities from the experiment, and you'll get about a 39% chance for this to happen. A tester will need to verify the result which asks for another mind alignment and brings down the probabilities to 20%. Again, I don't claim that this number is statistically significant and describes a general success ratio, but whatever the precise figures the probability falls exponentially with the number of participants that need to have their minds aligned. Problems like this often don't come to light before development because they are subtle and hidden behind things perceived as more important such as the price of gold-plating per square inch. We think that we don't have to be precise about things that everyone understands during analysis, because it's common sense how to draw a star with a number of points. The rules for the surface area should be clear from basic geometry. Let's disregard all the weird answers and consider just the fact that some people in the experiment counted only outer points, and some counted both outer and inner points. How would you test whether the system works correctly if 12 was given as the number of points? Is the correct star the one on the left or one on the right in Figure 1.3?

Figure 1.3. Which one of these has 12 points?

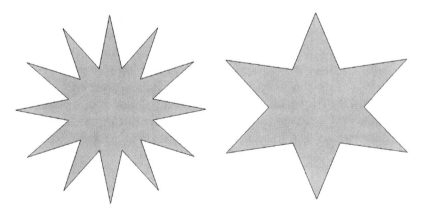

Things like this, where we feel familiar with the concept and implicitly think that others have the same understanding of it as we do, are one of the core causes of missing the target in software projects.

A small misunderstanding can cost a lot of money

The previous example was invented to demonstrate the point and arguably the misunderstanding is not a big one – the prices will be worked out correctly once everyone agrees on what a star with 12 points looks like. But the devil is in the detail. Wrong assumptions and misunderstandings that we have about the domain might not be huge, but they can still have a huge impact on the software that we deliver. Here is a real world example of how a tiny misunderstanding can cause a lot of pain.

Online poker is big business in UK at the moment, so loads of companies want to grab a piece of the action. Because poker is essentially a group game, potential newcomers are presented with a chicken-and-egg problem. In order for your poker system to be interesting to new players, it has to have lots of other players online. It is very hard to start up a network of players initially. Instead of attempting this, lots of UK bookmakers just make a deal with an existing poker network and then re-brand the software, instantly giving their customers many potential opponents and sharing a piece of the profit of the whole network. UK punters have accounts in British pounds but most poker networks work with US dollars as chips. So the system required a screen that allowed players to convert between UK pounds and US dollars. The requirement for this was to round the converted value to two decimal places, as a poker chip was worth one cent and fractions of cents were not supported. People who have worked on financial systems in the past probably already guess what happened.

This worked fine until one day someone found out how to make money out of it. For the sake of the story, let's say that the exchange rate was 0.54 pounds to a dollar. So 0.01 pounds would convert to 0.02 dollars, but a single cent would convert to a single penny – 0.0054 rounded to two decimals is 0.01. Because of the rounding, you could convert a single penny into two cents, then convert the first cent back to a penny, then convert the second cent into another penny and end up with twice the money you started with. Yes, it is just one penny more, but the guy who worked this out wrote a script to do the dirty job and apparently took more than ten thousand pounds before the fraud was discovered.

When the news about this broke, business people argued that the amount should have been rounded down and that the developers should have known this, but the developers argued that they received a request to round to two decimals without any specifics. The requirement to round to two decimals sounds obvious and unambiguous, just as did the question about the number of points in the star. In any case, the blame game does not solve the problem. We need to prevent problems like this by ensuring that developers and business analysts have the same understanding of 'rounding to two decimals'. The question needs to be raised before the development starts, not after it is in production, when someone finds a hole in the system.

Fulfilling specifications does not guarantee success

The communication gap on software projects doesn't only cause people to understand things differently. It also causes them to focus on unimportant issues. This is a huge source of problems. I have seen several projects where people wasted enormous amounts of effort building features that they thought were important, but in fact missed the real goals. Working from specifications does not guarantee that the project will deliver the desired business value.

Gilles Mantel organised a workshop entitled *Test-Driven Requirements: beyond tools*[5] at the Agile 2008 conference held in Toronto in August 2008. At the workshop, four volunteers acted as a customer, a product owner, a developer and a tester for a simple construction project involving children's play bricks and dominoes. (For the sake

---

[5]http://testdriveninformation.blogspot.com/2008/08/material-of-tdr-workshop-at-agile-2008.html

of the story, if you don't know what a product owner is, think of it as a business analyst.) There were two sets of construction bricks and dominoes, placed on two halves of a large table with a large white paper screen blocking the view in between, as shown in Figure 1.4.[6] A person sitting at one side of the table could not see anything on the other half. The aim of the workshop was to demonstrate how the requirements and testing processes fail when communication is impeded, even with something as simple as a domino construction.

At the start of the workshop, the product owner, the developer and the tester left the room. Mantel put together a simple construction on one half of the table with the customer, aligning the dominoes so that they all fell when a small lead ball was rolled down one of the bricks and bounced against another brick then the first domino. There were lots of other bricks in the construction, but *the primary business goal was to make all the dominoes fall when the ball was rolled.*

The product owner then walked into the room, looked at the construction and discussed it with the customer. Then the developer and the tester walked into the room. The developer was placed at the other half of the construction table, unable to see the original construction. The tester was placed on a different table, facing the construction table backwards and unable to see what was going on. This was intended to simulate the situation where a product owner acts as a customer representative and testers have no influence over development.

The product owner then started explaining to the developer how to replicate the construction. The developer started building with the bricks on his part of the table and the tester listened in to the conversation. The developer was allowed to ask any questions and the product owner was allowed to explain the construction in any way he saw fit, but the tester was not allowed to ask any questions during the construction. She just listened in and took notes. The product owner led the developer by explaining the shape and relative positions of different building blocks. They discussed at length

---

[6]The photograph is © Eric Lefevre, used with his permission

differences in colour and number of blocks. When the developer had finished building the system, the tester was asked to validate what the developer had built and approve or reject the release, without looking at the original construction. Based on her notes, the tester found a few issues and refused to approve the release. Gilles Mantel then performed the only test that was really important – he rolled the ball down the first brick. It did not bounce off the second brick and the dominoes did not fall.

Figure 1.4. Domino construction exercise at Agile 2008

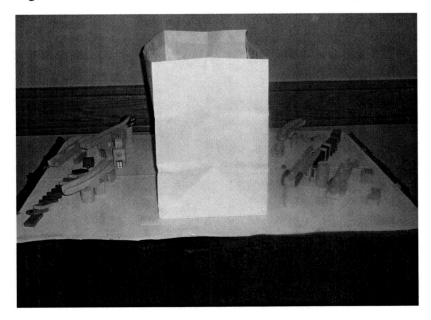

The interesting thing was that the product owner never asked the customer about the goal of the construction, so he was not able to communicate anything in this respect. This was not forbidden by the rules of the game, it just never happened. When the exercise ended, the customer said that the ordering of dominoes, alignment of bricks by colour and all the extra bricks on the table were not really important and that he would have accepted the construction if these were different providing the dominoes fell after the ball was rolled.

Unfortunately, the product owner and the developer wasted most of the time discussing exactly these issues and the tester validated the construction based on this discussion.

This exercise demonstrated very clearly what happens with the traditional requirements process, when the important business goals are simply lost in translation and lots of effort is wasted on irrelevant details. The developer had no real chance of fulfilling the business goal because he had no idea what it was.

The tester was just asked to approve or reject the release without really understanding what the project was about, based just on the specification put together by the product owner. So her contribution was left to pure chance as well. She did reject the release, but for the wrong reasons. In this case, it was lucky that the developer did not build the construction exactly as the product owner required, otherwise the tester would have approved the release. The result would have been correct in terms of the specifications, but would have completely missed the business goal.

Describing *how* and *what* but not *why* left the success of the project to pure chance. Instead of producing traditional specifications and requirements, we should really focus more on getting the communication right. Involving developers and testers from the start, communicating business goals to everyone and removing communication obstacles is the way we can take control of projects, and not leave success or failure to pure chance.

Requirements are often already a solution

Classical project requirements focus on *what* but not on *why*. They are effectively a proposed solution to a problem, but do not tell us what the problem actually is. Customers and business people who specify requirements generally have a very superficial view of software, which is hardly surprising as it is natural for them to focus on business rules and user interfaces and not on the infrastructure to support it. Because business people lack deeper technical understanding of implementation details, their proposed solution is sometimes much more complicated than it needs to be. It it is not uncommon for a technical person to suggest a much simpler solution once they know what the problem is.

In 2005, I was involved in building a J2EE-based system for Bluetooth content distribution. It was initially used for pushing small files and text messages to mobile phones. After a few months, the client wanted to add on-demand content pull and distribute large animations and video files. Enabling on-demand content pull required significant system changes, not to mention the fact that a Bluetooth network is not suitable for sending five-megabyte movie files to hundreds of mobile phones at frequent intervals. As always, the client wanted it done as soon as possible, ideally in less than two months. There was no way that such functionality could be implemented and work properly in time. Even if it was possible, such a hack would make future support a nightmare.

We asked the clients to identify the problems they wanted to solve by pulling films to the phones. It turned out that they had an opportunity to sell the system to an art fair, where the visitors would use mobile phones to view a video tour. From this perspective, the video tour had absolutely nothing in common with the original solution, except the idea of software running on mobile phones. We decided to build a small stand-alone application for the mobile devices, which would read all the files from an MMC memory card and would not communicate with any servers at all. This was done in time for the art fair and did not break the architecture of the server.

This example demonstrates how important it is to get technical people involved in the specifications process and to share information about the problems that we are trying to solve, not just the proposed solutions. Traditional ways of defining requirements and specifications only harness the knowledge of a selected few individuals, and don't really use all the brains on the team.

Both traditional and agile development processes expect clients and business experts to specify what the system should do and rely on them to get it right. I do not agree with this. Business experts and clients should definitely be in the driving seat of projects, but I think that much better results can be achieved if developers and testers also have a say in what is to be built.

Cognitive diversity is very important

Getting different people involved in the process of specifying the system is also very important from the aspect of cognitive diversity. When everyone in the group approaches a problem from a similar viewpoint, ideas are reinforced by a kind of echo effect and it becomes really hard to see blind spots. People in homogenous groups often tend to make decisions to minimise conflicts and reach consensus without really challenging or analysing any of the ideas put to discussion. In psychology, this effect is known as *groupthink*.[7] Groupthink is a serious problem for decision making, not limited to the software world. In *The Wisdom of Crowds*[6], James Surowiecki blamed major US foreign policy mistakes, such as the Bay of Pigs fiasco and the failure to anticipate the attack on Pearl Harbor, on overly enthusiastic plans as a result of Groupthink. Instead of making people wiser, Surowiecki claims that being in homogenous groups can make people dumber (see [6] pp. 341).

Small homogenous groups also exhibit the effects of peer pressure and conformity. Surowiecki quoted an experiment by Solomon Asch, in which he showed groups of people three lines and asked them to identify which line was the same length as a line on a card. Asch lined up people in the group and showed them a range of cards in sequence, asking them to give their answer out loud in the order they were lined up. Unknown to the last person in the line, all the other subjects had been actually told up front which answer to give. For the first few cards, they gave the correct answer and then deliberately started selecting incorrect lines. The last person then often started scrutinising

---

[7] http://en.wikipedia.org/wiki/Groupthink

the picture more, moving around to measure the lines again. About 70% of the subjects changed their answer at least once and one third of the subjects went along with the group at least half the time. Asch repeated the experiment with at least one of the collaborators selecting the correct answer. This immediately encouraged the experiment subjects to say what they really thought and "the rate of conformity plummeted". This experiment demonstrates the effects of peer pressure and how people are generally reluctant to state their opinion if it is contrary to all the other opinions in the room. It also demonstrates that the situation changes dramatically even when a single different opinion exists.

Surowiecki also states that even small groups of five to ten people can exhibit what he called the wisdom of the crowds, reaching a state where the group together is smarter than any individual in the group. Cognitive diversity and independence of opinion are key factors in achieving this. People should think about the problem from different perspectives and use different approaches and heuristics. They should also be free to offer their own judgments and knowledge rather than just repeating what other people put forward. By getting different people involved in the specification process, we can get the benefits of this effect and produce better specifications.

Breaking The Spirit of Kansas

On 23 February 2008 a B-2 stealth bomber named The Spirit of Kansas took off from from Andersen Air Force Base on the island of Guam. By that time, The Spirit of Kansas had more than 5000 flight hours and B-2 bombers were considered highly successful, having taken part in various military campaigns since 1999. Shortly after take-off, the plane started spinning and crashed inexplicably. The aircraft was completely destroyed, with an estimated $1.4 billions' worth of damage. The two pilots ejected in time and survived the crash with burns. On June 6th 2008, CNN reported[8] that the bomber crashed because of an issue with control instruments, caused by specific

---

[8]http://edition.cnn.com/2008/US/06/06/crash.ap/index.html

climate conditions over the island of Guam. Moisture caused three out of the plane's 24 sensors to receive distorted data, causing the flight-control system to send an erroneous correction command. The pilots and crew followed the right procedures and CNN quoted Major General Floyd L. Carpenter, who headed the accident investigation board, as saying that "the aircraft actually performed as it was designed. In other words, all the systems were functioning normally". Carpenter also said that some pilots and maintenance technicians had known about these specific climate issues for at least two years but had failed to communicate them. One of the conclusions of the investigation was that the human factor of failure to communicate critical information was one of the causes of the incident.

Although I was never involved in software crashes of this financial proportion, it was not uncommon to find that someone in the organisation had knowledge that could prevent a problem from happening in the first place, but they failed to communicate it. Facilitating communication throughout the project is a key factor for preventing major failures, but the traditional project model does not encourage this. Testers in particular may be aware of some problems that need to be addressed in development, but they do not get involved in the effort until very late and there is nothing that facilitates the extraction of such key knowledge from them with traditional specifications or requirements. This is not a problem specific to software projects, and lots of organisations struggle with extracting knowledge from their own employees. Lew Platt, a former CEO of Hewlett-Packard, is famously quoted for saying that "If HP knew what HP knows, we would be three times more profitable".[9]

 ## *Stuff to remember*

- The traditional specifications and requirements processes now established in the software industry are inadequate and essentially flawed.
- Specifications do not contain enough information for effective development or testing, they are prone to

[9]See *A Measurable Proposal* by Tom Davenport[7].

ambiguity and they only use the knowledge of a selected few individuals.

- Things get lost in translation between customers' original problems and development.
- Teams that do use agile development practices are affected by this problem less than those that do not use agile development practices, but they still suffer from it.
- Unless everyone involved understands the business goals, there is a high risk of missing the target.
- Developers and testers may skip or misinterpret parts of the specifications, and there is no easy way to check which parts are actually affected.
- Requirements are often already a proposed solution to the problem, and do not explain why something is required.
- Gaps and inconsistencies in traditional specifications get discovered only when developers start writing code.
- Change requests may introduce inconsistencies into the software, and there is no easy way to spot problematic rules and affected parts of the system.
- Specification documents often do not reflect the true state of implemented software.
- Customers and business analysts are expected to get the requirements and specifications right and the knowledge of developers and testers is not taken into account.
- The cumulative effects of small misunderstandings cause huge problems, but there is nothing to help us discover and resolve these issues before implementation.
- Matching what clients expect is essentially a communication problem, not a technical one.
- There are some things that are so obvious to the customer that she will never tell you them unless you ask.

Chapter 2
Finding ways to communicate better

In order to bridge the communication gap, we need to work on bringing business people and implementation teams together rather than separating them with formal processes and intermediaries. Ron Jeffries said, during his session on the natural laws of software development at Agile 2008, that the most important information in a requirements document are not the requirements, but the phone number of the person who wrote it. Instead of handing down incomplete abstract requirements, we should focus on facilitating the flow of information and better communication between all team members. Then people can work out for themselves whether the information is complete and correct and ensure that they understand each other.

Challenging requirements

Since requirements, however clearly expressed, may contain gaps and inconsistencies, how do we fight against this problem before development rather than discovering it later? How do we ensure that requirements, regardless of their form and whether or not they are built up incrementally before every iteration, are complete and correct? Donald Gause and Gerald Weinberg wrote in *Exploring Requirements*[3] that the most effective way of checking requirements is to use test cases very much like those for testing a completed system. They suggested using a black-box testing approach during the requirements phase because the design solution at this point still does not exist, making it the perfect black box. This idea might sound strange at first and it definitely takes a while to grasp. In essence, the idea is to work out how a system would be tested as a way to check whether the requirements give us enough information to build the system in the first place. We should not dive straight away into how to implement something, but rather think about how the finished system will be used and then double-check the requirements armed with this knowledge. Black-box test scripts are by nature very precise and contain clearly defined steps and values, unlike traditional requirements which are generally a lot more abstract.

On the timeline of a software project, requirements are at the very beginning and black-box tests are traditionally at the end. All the things in between make it hard to see a very subtle relationship between these two concepts. They effectively talk about the same thing: how the system will be used once it is developed. In fact, because tests are very precise, they offer a lot less chance for misunderstanding than abstract requirements. This makes tests theoretically an option for replacing requirements altogether. Robert C. Martin and Grigori Melnik even consider them the same thing in their *equivalence hypothesis*[8]:

> As formality increases, tests and requirements become indistinguishable. At the limit, tests and requirements are equivalent.

We really communicate with examples

In order to identify requirements, business analysts often work through a number of realistic examples with the customers, such as existing report forms or work processes. These examples are then translated to abstract requirements (equivalent to the the first step of the telephone game). An interesting thing about examples is that they pop up several times later in the process as well. Abstract requirements and specifications leave a lot of space for ambiguity and misunderstanding. In order to verify or reject ideas about the requirements, developers often resort to examples and try to put things in a more concrete perspective when talking about edge cases to business experts or customers. Concrete realistic examples give us a much better way to explain how things really work than requirements. Examples are simply a very effective communication technique and we use them all the time; this comes so naturally that we are often not aware of it. Test scripts that are produced to verify the system are also examples of how the system behaves. They capture a very concrete workflow, with clearly defined inputs and expected outputs.

The participants of the second Agile Alliance Functional Testing Tools workshop, held in August 2008 in Toronto, came up with a diagram[1] explaining the relationship between examples, requirements and tests shown in Figure 2.1. Examples, requirements and tests are essentially tied together in a loop.

Figure 2.1. Relationship between examples, tests and requirements

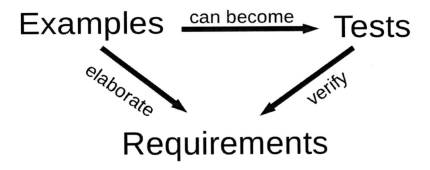

This close link between requirements, tests and examples signals that they all effectively deal with related concepts. The problem is that every time examples show up on the timeline of a software project, people have to re-invent them. Customers and business analysts use one set of examples to discuss the system requirements. Developers come up with their own examples to talk to business analysts. Testers come up with their own examples to write test scripts. Because of the effects illustrated by the telephone game, these examples might not

---

[1]Many thanks to Jennitta Andrea for pointing this out to me

describe the same things (and they often do not). Examples that developers invent are based on their understanding. Test scripts are derived from what testers think about the system.

Going back to the equivalence hypothesis, tests and requirements can be the same. Requirements are often driven from examples, and examples also end up as tests. With enough examples, we can build a full description of the future system. We can then discuss these examples to make sure that everyone understands them correctly. By formalising examples we can get rigorous requirements for the system and a good set of tests. If we use the same examples throughout the project, from discussions with customers and domain experts to testing, then developers or testers do not have to come up with their own examples in isolation. By consistently using the same set of examples we can eliminate the effects of the telephone game.

Working together, we find better solutions

Here is an example that shows how communication across project roles can lead to a better solution. During the Crevasse of Doom[2] presentation at the QCon conference in London in March 2007, Dan North talked about a project in the early days of Java, when printing documents was extremely hard to implement properly. The developers told the business people that all the requirements could be easily implemented, apart from those related to printing because printing APIs were not mature enough. The business people refused to give in because "printing was embedded in the core of their business". While discussing this further and talking about how exactly printing was embedded in the core of the business, the developers discovered that the users entered data in a screen, printed out the results of calculations, opened a different screen and entered these results, processed and printed results again, entered them in the third screen and so on. After seeing this, the developers suggested automatically

---

[2]http://www.infoq.com/presentations/Fowler-North-Crevasse-of-Doom

transferring the information between screens, invoking the amazed response "You can do that?". Although this example is rather simplistic, it illustrates a very important fact: neither group could solve the problem on their own, but together they found a great solution. The business users were so used to working around a technical difficulty that they really thought of printing as something embedded in the process. The developers did not really understand what was going on or why printing was needed.

If we help each other understand the goal better, then we will come up with better solutions. This is why building a shared understanding of the goal is one of the key practices in software development.

Communicating intent

The communication of goals was at the core of Prussian military tactics as a response to the dangers posed by Napoleon's invincible army. The Prussian leaders figured out that they did not have a single person capable of defeating Napoleon's genius, so they focused on allowing the individual commanders and their troops to act collectively to better effect. They made sure they told the commanders why something needed to be done and they put this information into the perspective of overall goals, rather than just passing down a list of imperative commands. The resulting military doctrine was called Auftragstaktik, or mission-type tactics, and it was key to the great successes of Prussian and later German armies. Today it survives as Mission Command in the US Army.

A key lesson to take from this and apply in software development is that understanding business reasons behind technical requests is crucial for building a shared understanding of the domain. Examples in the previous section and the section *Requirements are often already a solution* on page 18 demonstrate this. *Original intent is one of the most important things that a customer or a business analyst should pass on to the developers and testers.* At the same time, in my experience, passing on this information is one of the most underestimated and neglected practices in software development. This is just as much a problem in other areas. Going back to the example with US Army orders from the section *Imperative requirements are very easy to misunderstand* on page 8, effectively communicating the intent was one of the biggest problems that researchers identified. Gary Klein cites research by William Crain,[3] who found that only 19% of commanders' intent statements had anything to say about the purpose of the mission and that "communication of intent was mediocre". When domain experts reviewed the statements, the average score for effectiveness was below the average, "closer to very ineffective".

I was recently involved in a project where the clients said that they wanted real-time reporting on transactions in a highly distributed system. The system was being developed for batch reporting and introducing real-time reporting required a huge redesign, possibly even a major change to the infrastructure. Instead of challenging this requirement, the CTO of the company started to design a solution on the spot, immersing himself in a tough technical problem which, for him, was a pleasure to play with. I asked what the clients wanted to achieve with real-time reports and we came to the conclusion that they wanted to present up-to-date information to their partners during the working day, not just overnight. A delay of one hour was perfectly acceptable for this, without the need to redesign the system from scratch or invest a lot of money in real-time infrastructure, especially since real-time reporting on live transactional data would have seriously impacted the performance of the transaction processing service. In this case, the issue was with the meaning of word 'real-time'. For the customers, it meant 'updated several times per day' but for programmers it meant 'millisecond correctness'.

The moral of this story is that requirements should not really be taken at face value, especially if they come in the form of a solution that does not explain what the intent is (see the section *Requirements are often already a solution* on page 18). Teams often consider requirements as something carved in stone that has to match exactly what the customers demand. In fact, customers will often accept a different

---

[3] See page 225 of [4] and http://handle.dtic.mil/100.2/ADA225436

solution if it solves the problem, especially if it is a lot cheaper and easier to implement.

Understanding why something is required, instead of just blindly following instructions, is definitely one of the key factors for improving the chances of success in a software project. *This is why it is crucial to communicate the reasons behind technical requests and business decisions.* Don't be afraid to ask 'why' if you do not understand a requirement or if you find it strange.

Agile acceptance testing in a nutshell

We can bridge the communication gap by communicating intent, getting different roles involved in nailing down the requirements and exploiting the relationships between tests, examples and requirements. We can use realistic examples consistently throughout the project to avoid the translation and minimise the effect of the telephone game, saving information from falling through the communication gaps. In order to ensure that the initial set of examples is good enough for development and testing, programmers and testers have to get involved in defining them. The discussion about these examples builds up a shared understanding of the domain, flushing out small communication problems straight from the start.

This is essentially what agile acceptance testing is about. Over the years, it has evolved into a relatively simple and elegant practice. (Please do not confuse simple and elegant with easy. Implementing agile acceptance testing can be a real organisational challenge and may require a lot of effort. But it will pay off in a big way at the end.) It revolves around the following five ideas:

1. Use real-world examples to build a shared understanding of the domain.
2. Select a set of these examples to be a specification and an acceptance test suite.

3. Automate verification of the acceptance tests.

4. Focus the software development effort on the acceptance tests.

5. Use the set of acceptance tests to facilitate discussion about future change requests, effectively going back to step 1 for a new cycle of development.

Use real-world examples to build a shared understanding of the domain

Instead of abstract requirements that can easily be misinterpreted, we should talk about what the system does or should do in real-world situations. Abstract definitions can obscure our view and leave many ambiguities. Real-world examples do not suffer from this. Discussing realistic situations helps flush out assumed business rules and points us to the true business rules. Ideally, we want to identify representative cases that show all the differences in possibilities and then discuss these cases and how the system should behave. Writing the examples down on a whiteboard, wall, word document or a piece of paper will help discover gaps and identify additional scenarios and examples that we have to discuss. Working with real-world examples helps us communicate better because people will be able to relate to them more easily. It is also easier to spot inconsistencies between realistic examples. Developers, business people and testers all need to participate in the discussion about examples. Developers learn about the domain and get a solid foundation for implementation. Testers obtain the knowledge they need firsthand and they can influence the development by suggesting important cases for discussion. I explain this step in greater detail in Chapter 3 and Chapter 4.

Select a set of these examples to be a specification and an acceptance test suite

Once we have identified enough examples for everyone to be comfortable with starting the implementation, we can actually use the examples as the acceptance criteria for the current iteration of development. A selected set of examples can become the target for development – effectively the solution specification. Once the system does exactly what we discussed in all of the cases, it is ready to be shipped. Verifying all the cases becomes the final check-point before a release. This step is explained in greater detail in Chapter 5.

Automate verification of the acceptance tests

If we are moving away from the target, I'd like to know this sooner rather than later. So we want to be able to check the examples often, to make sure that the code is going towards the target. The biggest expense in software development today is the time of the implement-ation team members (again, I'm using this as a name for all parti-cipants in the development process, not just developers), so verifying the examples must not take a lot of time. In addition, automated tests provide quick feedback and make the rest of our work more efficient. This is why we need to automate the verifications. When all the examples are automated, we can check whether the code does what we expected with a touch of a button. This step is explained in greater detail in Chapter 5.

Focus the software development effort on the acceptance tests

At the end of the project all the examples should work. Because we ideally have a complete set of examples, if all the examples work there is nothing else that should be developed. So we can actually focus the development on satisfying the examples. After the examples are automated, we can verify the code quickly and often. Develop a bit of code to satisfy an example, run the verification and check whether we are really doing it correctly, then move on to the next example. This helps to avoid just-in-case code, which is what happens when developers have to think about all the edge cases to satisfy an abstract requirement. There are no abstract requirements, and we have examples to describe all the edge cases. When all the examples are implemented so that the system works as they describe, the job is done. To developers this might sound similar to unit testing, because it essentially tries to do the same thing on a higher level (but acceptance tests are not a replacement for unit tests). I talk about this step in more detail in Chapter 6.

Use the acceptance tests to facilitate future change

Once the development is done, change requests will start coming in. We can use the set of acceptance tests for previous phases of development as a relevant authoritative document on the system. We use them to discuss change requests and quickly discover conflicting rules and changes. This is explained in more detail in Chapter 7.

And repeat

These steps are continuously repeated throughout the project to clarify, specify, implement and verify small parts of the project iteratively and incrementally. In Chapter 8 I explain how this fits into the overall development process in more detail.

So what does testing have to do with this?

On the first page of the introduction I said that agile acceptance testing is a practice that improves communication in the team. I also talked about focusing development and producing better specifications. This often raises the question of what all this has to do with testing. In fact, the name agile acceptance testing is a bit misleading and one of the main causes for so many misconceptions about this practice. The name comes from the fact that this practice evolved from test-driven development (TDD). Don't confuse it with customer (or user) acceptance testing, which is a practice that was established a long time before agile acceptance testing. I explain the differences between these two later.

In test-driven development, developers write tests to specify what a unit of code should do, then implement the code unit to satisfy the requirement. These tests are called unit tests, as they focus on small code units. The benefits of this approach are a better focus on what the system should do and having a clearly defined target for development. The team can collectively own the code and verify it, so this practice facilitates better team work. Unit tests also hold the system together during change, allowing it to be more flexible. If a change unintentionally breaks some existing functionality, the relevant unit test will fail and alert developers about a problem.

The practice of unit testing was so useful that it was only logical to ask whether the same could be applied to business rules and drive whole phases of projects rather than just code units. Unit tests focus on code so they are completely in the domain of software developers. Business rules, on the other hand, should not be defined by developers. They have to be defined by domain experts and customers. But business domain experts rarely understand programming languages, so using the same tools to drive implementation of business rules and code units typically fails. Developers could write business rule tests with unit test tools, but these tests would only reflect what developers understand and they would still be affected by all the communication problems presented in Chapter 1. In order to get the best specifications, customers and implementation teams have to work together. There is simply no way for a business person to verify that a developer's test describes the end goal correctly with unit test tools. So, in theory, the ideas behind unit testing could be applied to business rules as well, but in practice the tests are impossible to communicate.

To solve the problem, better ways for specifying and automating tests for business rules were needed that could also be used to communicate with business people. Such tools would have to focus on capturing the customers' view of what the system should do when it is finished, effectively the functional acceptance criteria for the project. Then we could apply unit testing ideas by developing code to satisfy tests and running these tests to verify that the code is on target, then repeating the process until all tests go green. This is where the name agile acceptance testing comes from. This practice started by expanding the unit testing ideas to business rules, effectively specifying the acceptance criteria in a form that could be executed as tests on the code.

Going back to the conclusion of the previous chapter, the problem is essentially a communication issue, not a technical one. The biggest obstacle for any such effort is communication, so easy communication and collaboration with business people have to be part of any viable solution. Out of the effort to solve the problem have come tools like FIT, FitNesse and so on. The ideas applied in these tools solved the communication problem so nicely that the practice of agile acceptance testing evolved into a great way to build a shared understanding of the domain and enable all project participants to speak the same language. Testing, in any possible meaning of this word, becomes relatively unimportant because the greatest benefit is improved communication.

Today, the name of this practice itself has become a major obstacle to its adoption. The chief business analyst of a company I recently worked with just rejected getting involved in the practice, with the explanation "I do not write tests". The word testing unfortunately bears a negative connotation in the software development world. In all the companies I worked for, testers were among the least well-paid employees, right down there with the support engineers. Starting a discussion on testing somehow seems to give business people the green light to tune out. It is like a signal that the interesting part of the meeting is over and that they can start playing Sudoku or thinking about more important things. After all, testing is not something that they do.

The practice of agile acceptance testing, especially as a way to improve communication between team members and build a shared under-standing of the domain, relies on the participation of business people. They are the ones that need to pass their domain knowledge on to programmers and testers. They are also the ones that need to make decisions about edge cases and answer tough questions about business rules. So they very much have to 'do tests'.

To add a further complication, there is also user acceptance testing, which sounds very similar to agile acceptance testing. User acceptance testing (UAT) is a phase in a software project where clients sign off a deliverable and accept it as complete. It can involve testing by end-users, verification from stakeholders that they are happy with the product and a whole range of other testing activities. Although you can verify the software during UAT using a successful run through an acceptance testing suite as one of the criteria, agile acceptance testing has very little to do with user acceptance testing. In fact, they are on completely opposite sides of a software project. User acceptance testing happens after development and it is often the final confirmation before money changes hands. It is performed by the clients or third-party agents. Agile acceptance testing happens before and during development and it is performed by the implementation team.

Some people call this practice acceptance test-driven development to signify that acceptance tests are used to drive the development, not just to verify the deliveries at the end. Others try to reduce the confusion between user acceptance testing and agile acceptance testing by avoiding the use of the word 'acceptance' and calling the practice functional test-driven development. This also signals the difference between code-oriented unit tests which are traditionally linked with TDD and functional (acceptance) tests. Three or four years ago, the name storytest-driven development was used to describe this practice, emphasising the fact that acceptance tests are related to user stories and not code, but it did not really catch on. Another variant is test-driven requirements, explaining that acceptance tests actually deal with requirements more than with development. Brian Marick calls these tests business-facing to emphasise that business people should be concerned with them.[4]

---

[4]http://www.exampler.com/old-blog/2003/08/21/

Better names

Dan North suggests using the word 'behaviour' instead of 'test',[5] as a way to clear up a lot of misunderstandings. Instead of test-driven development, he talks about *behaviour-driven development* to avoid the negative connotation of testing. This trick has solved the problem of keeping business people awake quite a few times for me as well. Behaviour-driven development (BDD) is just a variant of agile acceptance testing, in my opinion. Some people will disagree, pointing out the differences in tools and format of test scripts. For me, the underlying principles are the same and BDD tools are just another way to automate tests. BDD also promotes a specific approach to implementation,[6] but this is not really important for the topic of this book. Again, I consider tools and tests to be of less importance than communication and building a shared understanding.

A name that has become more popular recently is *example-driven development*, with tests being called *specification by example*. This reflects the fact that we are using concrete real-world examples to produce the specifications instead of abstract requirements. I also like *executable specifications* as a name instead of acceptance tests, because it truly describes the nature of what we are building. Agile acceptance tests are specifications for development in a form that can be verified by executing them directly against the code.

People have tried to rename agile acceptance testing several times, but this name has somehow stuck. Most still use this name and this is why I decided to keep it here. I mention all the alternative names here because they are interesting attempts to remove the word 'test' from the vocabulary to reduce the ambiguity and misunderstanding that come from it. If your business people don't want to participate because testing is beneath them, try to present the same thing but with a different name.

---

[5] http://dannorth.net/introducing-bdd
[6] See http://behaviour-driven.org/ for more information

In any case, I want to point out that there are a lot of different names and ideas emerging at the moment, but they are all effectively different versions of the same underlying practice. This book is about the underlying values, practices and principles that all these names and ideas share.

 ## *Stuff to remember*

- Realistic examples are a great way to communicate, and we use them often without even thinking about it.
- Requirements, tests and examples all talk about the same thing – how a system will behave once it is delivered.
- We can use examples consistently throughout the project to avoid the effects of the telephone game.
- Building a shared understanding of the problem is one of the key practices in software development.
- Business intent is one of the most important things that a customer or a business analyst should pass on to the developers and testers.
- Cross-functional teams create much better specifications and requirements than business people in isolation.
- Agile acceptance testing uses these ideas to solve communication problems on software projects.
- The name agile acceptance testing is misleading but has been generally adopted.
- Agile acceptance testing is very different from user acceptance testing, and in general it is not about testing at all. It is about improving communication and building a shared understanding of the domain.
- Implementing agile acceptance testing can be a real organisational challenge.

Agile acceptance testing in a nutshell revolves around these five principles:

1. Use real-world examples to build a shared understanding of the domain.

2. Select a set of these examples to be a specification and an acceptance test suite.

3. Automate the verification of acceptance tests.

4. Focus the software development effort on the acceptance tests.

5. Use the set of acceptance tests to facilitate discussion about future change requests, effectively going back to step 1 for a new cycle of development.

Part II. Building and Maintaining a Shared Understanding

Using examples as specifications consistently throughout the project helps to avoid the effects of the telephone game and enables us to truly build a shared understanding of the system. In this part, we look into the roles of examples from specifications through development and testing to becoming a live documentation on the system. We also look into practices that enable us to get the most out of those examples.

Chapter 3

Specifying with examples

The first stage of agile acceptance testing is to make sure that we all know what we are talking about and more importantly to agree on this. Before a phase of development, be it an iteration, a mini-project or simply a chunk of software whose time has come, we specify what we expect out of it. We specify this in the form of real world examples, not with abstract requirements. The examples demonstrate how the system should act and how it should help users do their jobs. These examples are created by the whole implementation team, not by a single domain expert as in the traditional model. We use the examples to discuss the domain and make sure that there are no misunderstandings.

How do you brush your teeth?

Traditional requirements, even when written without functional gaps, leave a lot of room for misinterpretation because of hidden assumptions. People coming from different backgrounds see the same thing differently. They may not have the same interpretation when they read or hear something, as explained in the section *Are obvious things really obvious?* on page 9.

As a very effective demonstration of this, Mickey Phoenix asked people to describe how they brush their teeth at the Agile 2008 Conference in Toronto in August 2008, during his session on domain-specific testing languages.[1] Having proposed a very simple description such as 'put toothpaste on the toothbrush, open mouth, brush teeth...', he pointed out that the results of performing the first step might actually

---

[1] http://www.solutionsiq.com/agile2008/agile-2008-domain.php

look similar to the picture in Figure 3.1 to someone who has never seen a toothbrush before.

If we don't share the same understanding of the business domain, even the simplest of explanations can be ambiguous and misinterpreted. Software developers are technical experts and they know how to write code, but they often have no real experience of the business domain and their assumptions can be substantially different from the assumptions of business people. Unless we build a shared understanding and flush out assumptions, developers will often end up putting the toothpaste on the wrong side of the brush.

Figure 3.1. Put the toothpaste on the toothbrush

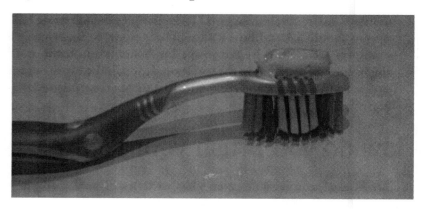

A live demonstration beats a list of instructions at any time – show people an example and they will learn a lot more and a lot faster. I noticed a short TV clip on one of the children's TV channels, which teaches viewers how to brush their teeth. Instead of just talking about it, the presenter demonstrated all the steps as he was explaining what kids should do. For those among you who will challenge this example for being overly simplistic and applicable only to children, here is something more relevant to adults in business. Try to explain how to tie a Windsor necktie knot only using words. I challenge you to explain it well enough so that someone can tie a correct Windsor knot based on your description. If you type 'Windsor knot' into the search field in Google, you will get loads of sites explaining how to tie the knot with images and even some videos – I have not found a single site in the first few result pages that does it only with words.

A practical example

One of the best ways to ensure that people understand each other is to demonstrate various differences in possibilities with realistic examples. In the poker example in the section *A small misunderstanding can cost a lot of money* on page 14, if there had been a discussion between developers and business people including the case where a cent is rounded to a penny, the business analysts would have spotted the issue straight away. Abstract requirements and specifications are not a good tool for communication. Real-life examples are much better.

Several years ago I was involved in building an affiliate advertising system. Affiliate advertising systems, for those of you who have slept through the web advertising revolution, connect web sites that want to advertise something and web sites that offer advertising space. The company that owns the web site with free space is called the affiliate. The company that sells products or services and wants to advertise pays a commission for the customers that come from the affiliate site by clicking on an advert. Today, the bulk of such commission is paid as a percentage of sales, but back then it was also paid on the number of clicks.

Our client wanted to build their own affiliate management system rather than join an existing ad exchange. For the sake of simplicity, let's say that their initial request was to pay affiliates 2 pounds, dollars or euros (whichever your preferred currency is) for 1000 clicks. As a requirement, 'pay 2 pounds per 1000 clicks' does not seem strange at all – in fact it is very much like any other normal requirement. However, although it seems precise, it leaves a lot of room for specu-lation. What happens if the affiliate has only 500 clicks on a particular day? Do we pay him 1 pound or do we not pay him anything at all? As a developer, I can think about this question and give an educated guess or opinion, but the real truth is that I should not be deciding about such an issue. This is a question for the business people because it is a manifestation of their business model. Maybe they want to pay a pound, maybe they want to wait for people to accumulate 1000 clicks. Both options are valid from a technical perspective, but there is only a single valid option from the business perspective. If we leave this question to developers to decide, there is a big chance that they will not select the same option as the customers did.

Problems like this one are not really bugs in the classical sense – they are caused by misunderstandings of business rules. The code might be completely correct from the unit testing perspective, but still miss the business target. This is where real-world examples come in. Instead of an abstract requirement such as 'pay 2 pounds per 1000 clicks', we need to identify interesting realistic cases and then discuss what happens in these cases.

For a start, it is very rare for a web site to get a nice round number of clicks. So a much more realistic case would be to have something like 7672 clicks during a day. What do we do with this number of clicks? Do we round it down and pay 14 pounds, or do we round it to 8000 clicks and pay 16 pounds? Maybe just scale it and pay 15.34 pounds? I like to throw in edge cases as well. Should we pay anything for 999 clicks? What happens with just one click? Discussing edge cases like these would have pointed out the problem with 1 cent in the foreign exchange story.

In this case, we could write the examples on a whiteboard, Excel spreadsheet or something like that and then identify the cases.

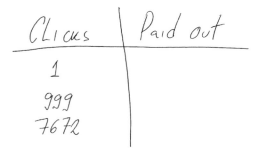

We then get the customers to give us values that they expect to pay in these situations:

CLicks	Paid out
1	0
999	0
7672	14

Discussing cases like these often raises more questions and reveals other interesting examples. Because we don't pay anything for 999 clicks, it is not really fair to the affiliates to simply ignore their total if they are missing a single click. In this case, the next question might be should we let the the 999 clicks roll over to the next day or do we reset the counter to zero for tomorrow? Maybe the clients are not too bothered with small web sites, they only want to focus on big advertisers who will have several thousands of clicks per day, so discarding this small remainder is not a big issue. Or maybe they also want to please the small advertisers, who will rarely have more than a thousand clicks on a day, but would appreciate being paid for the accumulated clicks. So we can create a few more examples on the whiteboard and discuss them:

DAy	CLicks	PAid Out
MONDAY	999	
Tuesday	10	

If we do allow the roll-over, then the example may raise additional questions. How many days do we allow the roll-over? What happens in the following case?

Day	Clicks	Paid out
Monday	999	
Tuesday	0	
Wednesday	10	

This may raise additional questions. Is there a limit to roll-over, a cut-off at the end of the month or something similar? Do we just let the clicks roll over and accumulate?

Although this example is a bit simplistic, this kind of process is very common once you start discussing realistic examples. Edge cases will lead to more questions, more examples, discussion, more questions and so on. The answers to all these questions depend on the customer's business model and they are not for the implementation team to answer, but it is their job to raise the right questions. The important fact is that these tough questions need to get asked and resolved before people start working on the code, not midway through implementing a class while the customer or business analyst is away and unreachable by phone. Just to make sure that there is no misunderstanding, I am not talking about having this discussion at the very beginning of an entire project. A workshop at the start of an iteration fits the 'before people start working on the code' criterion just fine.

Realistic examples make us think harder

Compared to abstract specifications or requirements, realistic examples offer a lot less chance for misunderstanding. We have to specify exactly how we want the system to work in a particular case.

Because examples get written down and discussed in detail, it also becomes easy to spot gaps, missing cases and inconsistencies that would otherwise have been noticed only during development.

While working through examples for a financial fraud detection system, I noticed that several of them had special cases for VIP customers. We then went back to the examples that did not have any special cases and asked whether the VIP status should be considered there as well. It turned out that several of these use cases (such as the freezing of funds) actually should not be applied to VIP customers. Problems like these would otherwise surface in production, after an angry call from a VIP customer. Discussing realistic examples allowed us to identify the gap and close it before the development started. I've heard an argument that this has nothing to do with working with realistic examples and that a good business analyst would have identified a problem such as this. I beg to differ. In this particular situation, there were eight people in the room among which four were domain specialists and one was an experienced senior business analyst. We all failed to spot the functional gap in the first round of analysis. Working with realistic examples made it much easier to spot that requirements were not consistent and provided a spark for the discussion. No matter how good a single person is, several people discussing realistic examples from different perspectives will flush out inconsistencies better.

Realistic examples contain precise information and they ask for precise answers. This often makes people think harder and not just brush the question off. It is not uncommon for people to disagree on edge cases during the discussion and actually fine-tune their business processes. I remember a situation where we discussed selling media clips online and asked what should happen if a customer wanted to buy a $10 clip but only had $9.50 in his account. Although the first response was that the sale should be refused, the CEO of the client company decided that it made more sense to allow the purchase to go through and to put the account into negative balance by 50 cents. This would increase sales and the customer would have to top up the account anyway before the next purchase. Developers and testers can sometimes provide a completely different perspective on a business problem.

Although I would not consider this situation as an example of how companies should create their business strategies, viewing things from a different perspective can sometimes help people spot new opportunities.

Identifying important examples

With agile processes, a feature is often implemented by incrementally adding functionality through several iterations. Mike Scott suggests[2] focusing first on a 'spine story' which contains the essence of a feature, and then adding details and exceptions in later iterations. Planning projects and splitting a feature into multiple iterations are subjects that are really beyond the scope of this book, but I do discuss them briefly in Chapter 9. For now, I want to point out that we need to focus on the examples that are really important for a particular phase of development, however it is planned. We should keep the future in mind in order not to paint ourselves into a corner, but it is important not to over-complicate things or to get bogged down in over-analysing all possible outcomes.

We want to gather as many representative examples as required to show all the possibilities and all the important cases for a feature for the current iteration. A good starting point is to take a description of a future piece of software, such as a use case, user story or whatever the unit of development in your planning method is, and then ask the customers "how should we verify that this piece of software is implemented completely and correctly?". Another question I often use is "pretend that it's magic and that we already delivered this thing – how would you actually test it?". Then these examples need to be written down, and discussed in detail.

We should then identify edge cases, negative paths and scenarios in which things do not go according to plan and discuss them as well. Far too often I've seen business people concerned with only the scenarios when everything is OK, leaving the negative cases for

[2]in a private e-mail

programmers to sort out. Again, you really do not want programmers to make decisions about your business model. Donald Gause and Gerald Weinberg ([3] pp. 251-2) suggest that a requirements test (which relates to a set of examples in agile acceptance testing) must consider the following three categories:

1. normal use
2. abnormal but reasonable use
3. abnormal and unreasonable use

'Unreasonable' in this case refers to something that a sane person would not do, but it can still realistically happen. These cases are most likely to be identified by testers because they think about breaking the system. Gause and Weinberg point this out saying that "No single failure of requirements work leads to more lawsuits than the confident declaration: No sane person would do *that*".

Team members often know about edge cases and potential problems and even know how to resolve them, but they need to communicate them effectively. Had the team members communicated their problems and concerns effectively, the plane described in the section *Breaking The Spirit of Kansas* on page 21 might still be flying. To avoid expensive crashes like these in our software, we should all focus on flushing out as many of these important examples as we can. Testers in particular are expected to suggest examples that demonstrate problems which they would typically check in later testing. In the next chapter, I introduce the specification workshop, which facilitates such a discussion.

If the example mentions numbers, I often throw in some numerical edge cases just to shake things up a bit and see if something interesting comes out. Reduce the numbers in the example by a very small amount, suggest some very small and very large figures. They will not necessarily lead to differences in processing, but may very well lead you to discover something that was missed the first time. Examples of this would be the 0.01 transaction in the foreign exchange example, 999 clicks in the web site advertising example and the media clip purchase for $9.50. When discussing very large or small amounts, ask first whether they are realistic or not. Keep in mind that there is a difference between unreasonable and unrealistic. We don't want to waste time discussing imaginary cases that are not important for the system.

Differences in similar examples

Watch out for differences identified in similar or related examples. Make sure to check whether any of the special cases should be considered for related examples as well. More often than not, this will help you discover gaps in the functionality. This is a lot easier to do when the examples are written down on a whiteboard or a wall, because you can see groups of examples together. Try to identify a common structure in the examples and write related examples close together in a similar form to spot such inconsistencies more easily. If the examples differ in one or two variables, then write them as a list or a table. Empty cells or combinations missing from the table might point you to more interesting cases.

Consider these few examples for an online flower shop that offers reusable free delivery vouchers to VIP clients when they make a single purchase over $50:

- Mark is a VIP customer. He puts a $50 flower arrangement in the shopping cart and goes to checkout. On checkout, he is offered free delivery since he is from the US.

- Mark has a previous unused free delivery offer. He puts a $30 flower arrangement in the shopping cart and goes to checkout. On checkout, he is offered free delivery.

- Mark has no previous unused free delivery offers. He puts a $30 flower arrangement in the shopping cart and goes to checkout. On checkout, he is only offered regular delivery.

- Lucy is a VIP customer from the UK. She puts a $50 flower arrangement in the shopping cart and goes to checkout, but she is offered only regular delivery since she is from the UK. We do not offer free delivery outside the US. We give her a free gift voucher instead.

- Tom is not a VIP customer. He puts a $50 arrangement in the shopping cart and goes to checkout. On checkout, he is only offered regular delivery.

The workflow steps and user names are not really important for these rules. Instead of writing down each scenario as a separate example, we could just have a single list that specifies something like this:

USER TYPE	COUNTRY OF RESIDENCE	ORDER VALUE	HAS UNUSED FREE DELIVERY OFFERS	OFFER FREE DELIVERY	SEND GIFT VOUCHER
VIP	US	50	No	YES	NO
VIP	US	30	YES	YES	NO
VIP	US	30	NO	NO	NO
VIP	UK	50	NO	NO	YES
REGULAR	US	50	NO	NO	NO

Writing things down like this makes it easier to spot some other interesting cases that need to be discussed. Obviously, we could write an example for a VIP customer from the UK that has only $30 worth of flowers in the cart. But there are some specification gaps that are less easy to spot, and the table uncovers them as well. For example, what do we do when someone has an unused free delivery offer, but they are a VIP customer and have more than $50 of flowers in the shopping cart? Do we keep the free delivery offer for the next time? What if they don't decide to use free delivery this time as well – do we allow them to keep two offers of free delivery for later or just one? What happens if for some reason a UK customer has a free delivery offer? How can this happen (perhaps we let someone change their address but keep a free delivery offer), and should we disable this option in this case? Ideally we want to flush out these important examples while we have business experts available to discuss them immediately.

Tables make it easy to spot differences

Those of you who have encountered FIT before will now surely notice how these tables can directly map to FIT acceptance tests (I discuss FIT in Chapter 10). At this point, I want you to disregard what you know about FIT or any similar tool, including your likes and dislikes. Even if you use a different tool that does not work with tables, do not throw away the baby with the bathwater. Think of tables primarily as a very good discussion-facilitating mechanism. Rick Mugridge and Ward Cunningham suggest that tables provide just enough structure to efficiently organise information, without getting in the way and over-complicating with formalisation ([9] p. 28). Tables were used to focus discussion and get better requirements long before agile acceptance testing and test-driven development were invented. David Parnas used them on the A-7 project for the US Naval Research Lab in 1977. He wrote about his experiences in 1996[10]:

> *Tabular notations are of great help in situations like this. One first determines the structure of the table, making sure that the headers cover all possible cases, then turns one's attention to completing the individual entries in the table. The task may extend over weeks or months; the use of the tabular format helps to make sure that no cases get forgotten.*

Regardless of how you write them down, working through a set of suggested examples will result in identifying new examples and interesting cases that were not covered by the initial set. This is perfectly normal and it is actually what we want. Be very suspicious if nobody identifies additional examples – this most likely indicates that people are not really participating.

Dealing with processing workflows

If the user story (or use case) contains some processing workflow, I like to draw the workflow on the wall or whiteboard and keep it there during the whole discussion. Decision points and processes in the workflow need to be discussed on their own, but keeping an eye on the big picture also helps to identify more important examples to discuss.

For example, Figure 3.2 is a picture of a bet placement workflow for an online betting system. Business people see this whole workflow as an integral process, but most of the boxes in the picture need to be discussed individually as they represent individual business rules.

Figure 3.2. Bet placement workflow

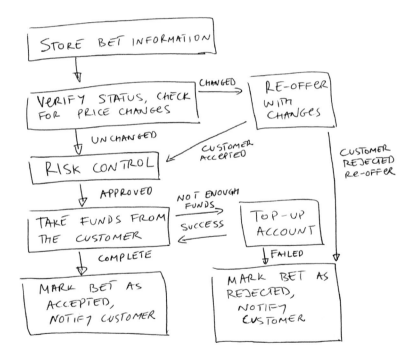

When we decompose a complex specification into a number of simpler specifications, we can focus better on each individual rule. For each of the decision boxes, there will be at least two or three important cases to cover. If we were to discuss everything as a single scenario, the number of important cases would be the product of the numbers of important cases at each decision point. In this example, this would be around 50 assuming that each step has two or three different important examples. If we discuss business rules individually, then the total number of cases is the sum of all important examples. In this example, this would be something between 10 and 15. These numbers apply only if we do not identify any important edge cases during the discussion, which is most unlikely. In a more realistic scenario, many edge cases would be identified and the difference between the numbers would be much larger. The combinatorial explosion effect makes all the many possibilities of a complex workflow really hard to describe and comprehend precisely. By focusing on individual rules within the workflow, we can have a much more meaningful discussion.

Depending on how you structure the deliverables of your project, it is not uncommon to implement individual steps in different phases or to different standards,[3] which means that not all examples need to be discussed at once. In this particular project, the automatic top-up of accounts could easily be put into the next phase of development and risk controls might not be implemented completely from the start. Drawing a big-picture diagram like this will help you see which parts may be postponed for later or implemented just partially.

Seeing the big picture is also important from the aspect of identifying functionality gaps. If three out of four decision points consider whether someone is a VIP customer or not, just ask whether the fourth decision point should be concerned with this as well. Maybe yes, maybe no, but let's make sure.

I do not advocate using any special or precise diagramming technique to draw the process. As long as everyone in the room understands what the diagram shows, any sort of drawing is fine. You can use UML, algorithm diagrams or just write steps in English and connect them with arrows. Don't use the discussion about examples as a chance to practice your UML skills if other people in the room do not understand UML.

---

[3] http://gojko.net/2007/12/04/waterfall-trap/

Working with business workflows

Sometimes a set of examples only makes sense in the context of a workflow and it is really hard to look at them just as a collection of rules. An example might be the sequence of steps in a wizard helper or a security alert escalation procedure. When dealing with such workflow examples, try to organise them in a way that clearly identifies what the preconditions are, what the workflow steps are and what are the expected outcomes of the workflow. Thinking in terms of these three aspects, sequenced in this order, will help you focus the discussion on a single rule and identify important issues around it. The behaviour-driven development scenario template is a useful way to write workflow examples down. It consists of three parts:

1. Given *preconditions*
2. When *actions* or *triggers*
3. Then *consequences*

For example, a simple scenario describing credit card transaction approval would be:

1. Given the customer has a balance of $0, and the customer has a deposit transaction for $10 and the transaction is in the authorisation state
2. When an AUTH-8440 message comes from the bank
3. Then the transaction is accepted and the customer has a balance of $10

I find that tables are more useful for expressing specifications, state machine transitions and calculation-based rules. The expressiveness of natural language and the sequential style of writing help to get a better understanding of the process for workflows. Again, this format may seem familiar to people who use BDD tools, but this is irrelevant. Even if you do not plan to use a BDD-style tool, try to write business workflow examples in this format because it will enable you to have a more meaningful discussion about them. Each flow example should focus on a single rule, so that the discussion can focus on this as well. If larger flows are written as a single example, it's often hard to keep track of the context and it becomes easy for ambiguity and hidden complexities to pass undetected.

Stuff to remember

- Instead of abstract requirements, use realistic examples to demonstrate differences in possibilities.
- The whole team should be involved in working through edge cases and resolving ambiguities.
- Discussing realistic examples makes people think harder and they are less likely to just brush questions off.
- Watch out for small differences in examples, as they might indicate that a business rule is not directly expressed.
- Write specifications down as tables to make it easier to grasp the content and spot gaps and inconsistencies.
- With processing workflows, discuss rules for each decision point separately.
- For genuine workflows, write down examples so that preconditions, processing steps and verifications are clearly separated.

Chapter 4
Specification workshops

Just writing the specifications or requirements as realistic examples instead of abstract sentences is not enough. To get the most out of realistic examples, we need to put them to an open discussion and give everyone a chance to review them and ensure that we all understand the same thing.

A customer or a product owner would typically be concerned mostly with the happy path, such as paying two pounds for every thousand clicks. Developers tend to focus much more on edge cases and alternative scenarios, so a developer might suggest an example with 999 clicks for discussion. Testers often think about how to break or cheat the system, so a tester might suggest the case where all 1000 clicks come from the same IP address in a time frame of five seconds. Do we still pay the affiliate in this case, or do we ignore it? A developer might then again ask what if this same affiliate had 3000 more clicks on the day – do we pay six pounds for these further clicks or do we ignore the affiliate completely?

All these people have different views of the system and ultimately different mindsets. This is why examples have to be put to discussion and analysed by the whole team. To facilitate this process, I like to gather customers, business domain experts, developers and testers around a whiteboard or a wall that we can write on and discuss interesting examples. If the team is small, then the whole team gets involved in this. With larger teams this might be a challenge because it is hard to keep ten or more people focused on a single thing. For larger teams, get at least one person from each of these groups in the room. At the start of an iteration, this turns into an intensive, hands-on problem and domain exploration exercise, driven by examples. I call this exercise the *specification workshop*. The workshop is focused on a particular piece of future development, a single iteration, and in it we try to iron out as many problems and identify and close as many functional gaps and ambiguities as possible.

In addition to domain specialists, testers and developers, it is ideal to have a project stakeholder present during each workshop as well. In fact, one of the most common mistakes with workshops is not including stakeholders. The goal of the exercise is to nail down scope. In order to do this, you need someone who has the ultimate say in what goes in and what does not go into the project, someone who controls the money. That person has to be there to resolve conflicts arising from potential scope creep as the domain is explored in detail and to provide provide the business's managers with feedback on what is in the specification.

The goal of the workshop is to build a shared understanding of the problem and the solution and to make sure that all the functional gaps are identified early, not later in the iteration, when business people might not be readily available. Senior business stakeholders and domain experts are typically bottlenecks for information transfer in software development, because they have both to do their own daily jobs and participate in the development project. The workshop makes effective use of their time, so that they can really focus on the issues and transfer their knowledge to the implementation team. For a two-week iteration, three or four hours are typically enough for a workshop. If you cannot explain what you want to build and get general agreement on it in four hours, this probably means that you will not be able to build it in two weeks.

Running a workshop

The workshop starts with a business person, typically the product owner, business sponsor or an analyst, briefly describing a piece of software that needs to be developed. He then explains how the code should work once it is developed, providing realistic examples. Other workshop participants ask questions, suggest additional examples that make the functionality clearer or expose edge cases that concern them. One of the main goals of the specification workshop is to flush out these additional cases before the development starts, while business people are immediately available to discuss them.

Discussing examples facilitates an efficient transfer of domain knowledge and provides a way for all the participants to ensure that they agree on the same thing. It builds a shared understanding of the domain. While discussing a use case, user story or whichever technique you use to describe requirements, it is the job of the developers and testers to raise all the tough questions and point out different examples. The job of the customers, domain experts and business analysts is to answer these questions and make sure that the other participants have understood the answers correctly.

Instead of just filling in the blanks in the examples, customers and business analysts should try to explain their decisions and make sure that others understand them. The specification workshop is the perfect chance to pass on domain knowledge to the implementation team and we should use this chance to help everyone build a common understanding. Knowing business reasons and understanding the domain might not give developers and testers the power to make business decisions, but it will give them enough knowledge to spot when something is suspect and enable them to communicate much more effectively with business people. Every once in a while, it also leads to much simpler solutions that satisfy the customers' needs.

For the specification workshop to be really effective, people should be free to challenge ideas and ask for clarifications until everyone really agrees and understands the same things about the domain. The specification workshop ends only when everyone involved agrees that they have enough examples to move on, that they have identified all important representative scenarios and covered all the edge cases.

Keeping one step ahead

To work more efficiently, business analysts may move one step ahead and work with the customers to identify and specify important examples for the next month's work. This is absolutely fine, but it must not be an excuse to skip the workshop at the beginning of this next iteration. The examples that the business analysts have written will be a good starting point for the workshop, but developers and testers need to understand them, identify and suggest missing cases and get a chance to discuss and critique the initial set of examples.

The workshop is especially important if there is no on-site customer representative sitting with the implementation team, as it then gives developers and testers regular planned access to domain experts. It is often not possible to have domain experts constantly available, but it should not be too hard to get them in the room with developers every second Friday for a few hours.

Make sure that you get answers from subject authorities

Mike Cohn wrote that the problem with business analysts acting as customer proxies is that they often try to answer questions themselves rather than researching the issue with users and customers ([11] chapter 5). A similar situation can happen with a direct customer representative if they are not an expert in a particular domain. On one of my recent projects we had direct access to a payment manager from the customer's organisation, and we relied on her completely to answer all payment-related questions. But she did not really know much about their security processes and when the time came to discuss fraud detection, we went through the first cut of examples with her and then asked her politely to verify the examples with the security managers.

If you are at all unsure about the answer, just write the case down and discuss it with business domain experts later. If a customer representative is not available, make sure to communicate the results with them and get their opinion on all the examples as well after the workshop. Try to elicit more interesting examples from them by asking whether you have covered all the important cases.

Sometimes the business people will look bored or uninterested when an example is being discussed. This is a huge warning signal and it might mean two things. The first is that the example is not realistic or not important for the scope of the system, in which case it should be thrown out. The second is that you are not talking to the right person. A call centre operator will have absolutely no opinion on background fraud screening, and if you try to talk to them about it they will probably just give you a blank stare. This is a signal that you should find someone who is interested in background fraud screening and talk to them about it, or get them involved in a different way.

Workshop output

The primary output of the workshop is a tangible set of realistic examples that explain how the system should behave once the next phase is complete. Key examples for every story or use case for the next iteration should be discussed, including the main success scenario and key edge cases. They should be explained and written down in enough detail so that all participants agree on what the story is, what are the deliverables and how to verify that they are correct. To keep the flow going, you might just take photos of whiteboards or have someone write down examples into text documents as you discuss them. It is not really important to have them in any specific format or tool, as there will be a time to clean them up later (we discuss this in the next chapter).

The key feature of these examples is that they should provide enough information for developers to implement and for testers to verify the stories planned for the iteration. The workshop should answer most of the questions about the specification that developers or testers would normally ask during the next few weeks of work. It is OK to leave some edge cases for later as long as the discussion during the workshop provides a framework to understand these cases. Make sure to discuss success scenarios and exceptions, but don't waste time specifying examples for all possible permutations of parameters. One example for each important case is enough.

To keep the workshop focused and keep the flow going, it is best to keep the examples and discussion on a fairly high level. We want to discuss *what* the software does, not *how* it does it. The discussion on *how* software implements something should take place later and does not necessarily need to involve project stakeholders or domain experts. Although possible implementations sometimes need to be considered during the workshop because they limit what can be done, as a general rule of thumb try to avoid talking about implementation or infrastructure details. This will save time and keep the flow going.

Sharing domain knowledge

There is one additional output, which is less tangible but I consider it even more important. The discussion about examples, edge cases and scenarios that takes place during the workshop enables developers and testers to learn about the domain. Not just learn, but ensure that everyone involved agrees and understands the same thing. In a sense, the process of getting to the list of examples that describe the desired behaviour is more important than the examples themselves. Donald Gause and Gerald Weinberg have a similar conclusion about their process for exploring requirements. Paraphrasing Dwight Eisenhower's famous quote about plans and planning, they said that the document is nothing, but documenting is everything ([3] p. xvi).

This note is important because people often focus on the tangible outputs and forget about the benefits of the discussion. A crucial role of the customer representative or business analyst during the workshop is to ensure that developers and testers gain a deep understanding of the problem, as well as get answers to immediate questions. The specification workshop is also a chance for developers and testers to get clarification on any issues that they have with the specification. The structure of examples provides a way to effectively communicate the differences in assumptions and expectations.

Feedback exercises

Donald Gause and Gerald Weinberg suggest using *ambiguity polls* to spot places where people disagree because of hidden assumptions and help them reach an agreement ([3] Ch. 9). Their ambiguity poll idea consists of selecting a metric that requires a solid understanding of the domain to estimate. This can be, for example, performance, cost or time to complete a task. The participants in the poll are asked to estimate the metric independently and then discuss the variations in results to grasp the reasons behind them. With a larger number of participants, these polls often have clustered results where clusters denote differences in understanding and variations in a cluster often relate to observational differences. Although most specification workshops I am involved in do not have nearly the number of participants required for numeric power laws to kick in, this idea is applicable to smaller groups as well. In fact, it is already used in agile planning and is known as *planning poker*. In planning poker, members of the implementation team are asked to secretly select a card that represents their estimate of how long it would take to develop a task. All cards are then shown at the same time and the people who had the highest and the lowest estimates explain their reasoning to the group. This often leads to the discovery of sub-tasks or constraints that the group was not aware of, or shortcuts that only a few people in the group know. The process is then repeated until the estimates converge. (Mike Cohn explains this in more detail in [12] Ch. 6)

A similar idea is described by Gary Klein in Sources of Power[4]. He suggested using *feedback exercises* to improve understanding between commanders and teams. In a feedback exercise, commanders first give orders as normal, and then the person running the experiment describes a potential unexpected event. The commander then writes down how the team should react and team members also write down what they would actually do. The notes are then compared and mismatches and surprises are used as a basis for discussion on how to improve communication.

We can use these ideas to improve mutual understanding during the specification workshop. Although the business people are the only ones who can give authoritative answers and make decisions during the workshop, other participants should be able to make good educated guesses if they all share the same understanding. Taking the core idea from ambiguity polls, we choose examples that require a deep understanding of the domain and ask the participants to work out how the system should behave and then explain the reasons behind their conclusions. The differences and mismatches can be used as a basis for further discussion and the building of a shared understanding of the domain. If you are evaluating a numerical output with a larger group, clusters of values might start showing up. The spread of estimated values tells us, in a sense, how much disagreement there is. Clusters indicate common sets of assumptions and these are also an interesting topic for discussion.

The opportunity to run these feedback exercises offered by specification workshops is one more reason why they are much more effective than if a single person writes examples or requirements. Gaining a deeper insight into the business domain will enable everyone to communicate more efficiently as the project progresses. Programmers who know the business domain will be able to spot inconsistencies easier and to help their colleagues resolve domain issues more efficiently. Testers learn about the domain and get involved from the start, so when the time comes for them to verify a deliverable, they will actually know what to expect and how to check it. This will allow them to do their job much more efficiently. Testers can also raise their concerns about potential problems before the development even starts, preventing problems.

Building a domain language

One of the biggest problems for effective communication on software projects is that programmers often come up with their own jargon. They use class names to refer to concepts and also frequently use technical terms such as names of design patterns and coding techniques. Business people use their own jargon to refer to the same concepts, often leading to a lot of misunderstanding and translation problems. I worked on a risk management system that involved assigning a particular set of risk assessments to an account. Business analysts called the set of assessments a risk profile. Programmers called it a risk template, because it was implemented as a template that they applied to create objects. They used the name risk profile for a particular instance of the template that was associated with an active account. This caused a lot of weird questions and explanations all the time.

A traditional solution for this problem is to have translators, people who speak both jargons. A team leader or a senior programmer eventually learns enough about the domain to be able to communicate with business people (or the project is definitely doomed). Sometimes a business analyst comes from a programming background so they know that a facade is not necessarily just an exterior wall of a building, but also the name of a popular software design pattern. These bilingual people then become major bottlenecks in communication and their interpretations are not always completely correct. Things often get lost in translation.

A much better solution is to avoid the need for translation altogether and make everyone use the same language from the start, a language that Eric Evans calls a *ubiquitous language* ([13] Ch. 2). Evans suggests intentionally selecting and evolving a language based on the domain model, which connects team communication to the software implementation. This language should then be used consistently throughout the project.

It is often much easier for the developers to speak the business jargon then to teach business people about programming abstractions and techniques, so we should start creating this language by using the names that business people normally use for concepts. After all, the goal of software is to solve a business problem so it makes a lot of sense to use the current business language. This does not mean that we are limited to existing words and phrases. The ubiquitous language is not dead, it is a living language and evolves with the project. To use it effectively, we will need to expand it with new concepts. The active use of the ubiquitous language will reveal gaps and awkward phrases, and we then need to create new phrases in the language to cover these cases and simplify the discussion. As we develop the model and implement more and more functionality, new concepts will be introduced into the system and we will expand the language with names for these concepts as well. But the important thing is to consistently use the same language. There must be no business jargon and technical jargon – just a single project jargon, the ubiquitous language.

The ubiquitous language should be used in all the examples, diagrams, code and speech. This involves the specification workshop, the discussion that takes place there and any documents that come out as a result. Examples that we use to build our specifications are a great way to start creating the language and to challenge and evolve it in practice. Enforcing the use of the ubiquitous language will make the specification workshop much more effective because it helps to reduce misunderstandings and ambiguity. At the same time, the workshop will point to new concepts and ideas, and we will need to find names for these new concepts. The specification workshop is a perfect place to discuss and agree on the names so that everyone understands them.

What specification workshops are not

A specification workshop is a very effective way to achieve a lot in a short time, but we need to keep it focused to get the benefits. If you notice that people have their laptops open and answer e-mail, write code or browse the web, the workshop has failed. This might suggest that people are simply too busy to do the workshop now, in which case you should reschedule it. Or it can signal that you have the wrong people in the room.

The workshop is not a meeting

It is very important to remember the goals of the workshop and focus on them, and not let the workshop diverge into yet another meeting.

I've organised workshops with a dozen people involved that were very effective, but it was a real challenge to keep everyone focused on the task in hand and not discuss other problems. This is why I think that smaller workshops are better. Two developers, two testers and a few business people should be enough to get the thing right. The developers can then use the examples that come out of the workshop to pass the knowledge on to other developers. Testers can do the same with other testers.

The workshop is not a presentation

A workshop should be an interactive collaborative effort to produce the complete set of relevant examples. It should not be the stage for a single person to present a monologue on his opinions of the system. There is nothing wrong with a single person driving the discussion, but there has to be a discussion for the workshop to be effective. Developers and testers should be encouraged to present their concerns and ask questions to clarify their understanding of the domain.

The workshop is not a design session

It is OK to explore possible implementations during the specification workshop to understand what is possible and to gain some deeper insight into the problem, but do not get distracted and go into detailed system design at this point. A specification workshop should be focused on *what* the system should do, not *how* how it will be implemented. It is a very good idea to have design workshops with business people and developers but they should be run separately and focus on design, not scope.

Effective design workshops look further into the future and explore different possibilities and ways to achieve the end-result when you know what you are building. They require the participation of domain experts and senior developers. Specification workshops help you to decide what exactly you want to build, and they should really be focused just on the upcoming iteration. They should include domain experts and senior developers as well as testers, stakeholders and the rest of the implementation team.

How to keep the workshop focused

If you are having trouble keeping the workshop focused, think about reducing the size of the workshop team or beginning by reaching an agreement on what will be discussed at the workshop. Declaring one person a facilitator of the workshop and giving this person the right to change the topic, provoke questions and stop people if they take over the show might be a good idea. The facilitator can then be charged with getting everyone involved in the discussion, eliciting questions and concerns from developers and testers and making sure that the discussion does not go astray. I will discuss this in much more detail in the section *Choose a facilitator for the workshops* on page 152.

In Sources of Power[4], Klein cites a paper by Karl Weick entitled *Managerial thought in the context of action*[14], which suggests a modified template for an effective commander's intent document:

1. Here's what I think we face
2. Here's what I think we should do
3. Here's why
4. Here's what we should keep our eye on
5. Now, talk to me

This list of topics is a very nice reminder for the discussion that needs to take place during an specification workshop, and it might be really useful to you if you are trying to act as a facilitator. The steps do not have to happen in the sequence described above and they should not happen by a single person lecturing or commanding the rest. We want to promote a collaborative discovery and learning effort, but we should cover all of them in the workshop so consider the list just as a good reminder of what to talk about.

Here's what I think we face

Applied to the specification workshop, this asks for a brief introduction of the next item for discussion by the facilitator or the person who contributed the item, explaining what the item is from his perspective so that others in the room can understand what exactly he is talking about.

Here's what I think we should do

Applied to the specification workshop, this asks for key examples to be identified and discussed. This will often start by the author of the business case explaining only the positive execution branch, sometimes with a few common negative cases. Don't stop there. Others should join in, identify and discuss all important examples using the techniques explained in the section *Identifying important examples* on page 50.

Here's why

Applied to the specification workshop, this asks for the business reasons behind a business case to be clearly communicated, discussed and explained to everyone. This will provide a better framework for understanding and may launch a series of challenges and questions ultimately resulting in a better overall solution than the basic set of examples would have.

Here's what we should keep our eye on

Applied to the specification workshop, this asks for potential problems and concerns to be identified and discussed. People rarely discuss these when planning an iteration of development. Things we should keep an eye on includes potential problems, things that we do not want to do (anti-goals) and possible misunderstandings, and keeping these in mind helps a lot to focus the development on the things that we really want to have.

Now, talk to me

The specification workshop should not be a lecture or a talk, it should be an open discussion. We need to make sure that everyone voices their concerns and has their questions answered (or written down and chased later). If some are not participating in the discussion, the facilitator should encourage them to join in.

Dealing with open issues

Working with real-world examples and writing them down will help flush out inconsistencies and identify gaps in requirements. This will facilitate the discussion and help clear up a lot of edge cases. However, some questions will inevitably be left open. The team might not have enough information to complete the example, or they might not be able to agree on what the system should do in a particular case. Some proposals will require the approval of a more senior stakeholder, or a decision from a particular business specialist not present at the workshop. It is important to identify, discuss and write down these incomplete questions, as well as the others. If there is a proposed outcome that needs verification, write this down too, knowing that it may not actually be correct. Then one of the team members (typically a business analyst if you have one) should resolve all the open questions with a senior stakeholder or a domain specialist. Discussing real-world examples will help business analysts communicate better with specialists or senior stakeholders, just as it does for workshop participants. The business specialist will not be able just to brush the question off or give a vague answer: a real world example with precise data requires a precise answer. Having a proposed outcome will help the specialists review the example and decide whether it needs to be corrected.

If a customer representative is not present during the workshop, then the examples must be reviewed by customers after the workshop. It is much better to have customers in the workshop, but sometimes this is not possible. The customer should review the examples and answer the unresolved questions. When the questions have been resolved, the examples should be updated to reflect the new insights. A second workshop to discuss the changes is often not required, unless the discussion with the specialist uncovers a large misunderstanding. It is often just enough to update the expected results and have other team members review them during the implementation.

 Stuff to remember

- Examples should be put to an open discussion and reviewed by all members of the implementation team.
- At the start of an iteration hold a specification workshop to discuss examples, iron out ambiguities and functional gaps and build a shared understanding.
- Developers and testers should suggest examples of edge cases or important issues for discussion.
- Make sure that domain experts and subject authorities answer questions. Don't make up answers yourself.
- Business people should explain their answers to make sure that others understand them correctly.
- The discussion that happens during the workshop is itself very valuable, because it teaches people about the domain.
- Organise feedback exercises to ensure that all participants share the same understanding.
- Create and use an ubiquitous language consistently in the workshop and all examples. Use the workshop to evolve the ubiquitous language.
- Keep the workshop focused, don't let it become just another meeting.
- Selecting a facilitator for the workshop can help to keep it focused.
- If a customer representative is not present at the workshop, make sure that they review and approve the examples.

Chapter 5

Choosing acceptance criteria

One very useful feature of realistic examples is that they are often easily verifiable. They have precise starting values and precise expected results. Once the software has been developed, we can actually check whether the system pays out 14 pounds after 7672 clicks or not.

We use the examples that come out of workshops, described in the previous chapter, to specify how a piece of software should behave once it is implemented and confirm that it actually does what we want it to do. Examples of system behaviour effectively become our acceptance criteria for the current phase of development.

Acceptance tests are the specification

We try to discuss all the different interesting and important cases during workshops. During this exploration exercise, there is often some duplication as we uncover different cases that actually describe the same business rules or find out that some of the parameters do not really have an effect on the outcome. We need to clean this up, select examples that represent all relevant differences in possibilities and formalise them into acceptance tests. This universally agreed set of acceptance tests becomes the specification for development. They should be used by developers as a target for what they need to do. They should also be be used by testers as part of their testing process. Business analysts and customers can use them to discuss open issues and revisit specifications when needed.

Some organisations work by requiring sign-off from key stakeholders at various stages of their development process. In general, I consider sign-off as a control measure that is there to ensure that someone reads the specifications carefully and as a stick to beat someone with when they want to change something later. The discussion during the specification workshop should provide a much better review of the specifications than any single person reading a huge document. Introducing changes later is no big deal with agile methods, especially if you use the examples as a live specification.

Save yourselves the trouble of maintaining and coordinating two sets of specifications and skip writing big requirements and specifications documents. Get clients to participate in specification workshops or to review the examples that come out of them. If you still want or need to get sign-off because of political or organisational reasons, then the acceptance tests are what you should get signed off. After each workshop, clean up the examples and print them in some formal document layout, then get the document approved by the stakeholders as the specification for the next iteration. If the name 'test' is causing problems for you in this respect, use one of the alternative names suggested in the section *Better names* on page 38. It might be easier to get a sign-off against an executable specification rather than a set of tests.

With workshops in place, tests tend to be fairly stable during the iterations, especially if they are focused on *what* the system should do and not *how* it should do it. If the iterations are short enough, the sign-off process for tests might work just fine. In practice, unless corporate politics really prevent this, I still would not treat the tests as something carved in stone and I would allow people to change them during the implementation.

Choosing the right set of examples

Our goal in each specification workshop is to explore various cases and seek to demonstrate differences in possibilities in order to facilitate discussion and learning about the domain. As suggested in the previous chapter, throwing in numerical edge cases, very small or large values and discussing challenges that testers or developers put forward may lead to interesting new examples, or it may just reinforce an already known rule. Therefore, the workshop often produces a number of examples that demonstrate identical rules. To make tests easier to read, understand and verify, we should select one representative example out of each such set and add it to the set of tests. If testers suspect that particular specific values are likely to cause bugs, add these examples as well, even though they might demonstrate a rule that has already been added to the tests. Having these as tests will make sure that the bugs do not appear in the code.

Naresh Jain has adapted the SMART acronym, typically applied to project goals,[1] for acceptance tests. Good acceptance tests, according to Jain, have these properties:[2]

- Specific – they are explicitly defined and definite
- Measurable – the result is observable and quantifiable
- Achievable – they describe a realistic scenario
- Relevant – they are related to the particular story
- Time-bound – the result can be observed almost instantly

Formalising examples into tests is the final phase in which we should iron out any ambiguities and inconsistencies. Writing things down in a formal way always helps to identify gaps. Ideally this should be done at the end of the specification workshop while the workshop participants are still in the room and ready to discuss any new issues. Alternatively, someone may take this task offline and write the set of tests based on examples discussed during the workshop, photos of whiteboard drawings and things that were written down on walls or paper. If the examples are formalised into tests after the workshop, I strongly recommend sending the final set of tests back to all the workshop participants and asking them to review it.

---

[1]http://gojko.net/2006/10/22/magic-of-goals
[2]http://www.slideshare.net/nashjain/acceptance-test-driven-development-350264

Distilling the specifications

In the section *Identifying important examples* on page 50 I said that the question 'how would you test this piece of software' is a very good starting point for the discussion during a specification workshop. When the result of the discussion is formalised into a set of acceptance tests, we don't really want to record all the details of the discussion. In order to get the most out of acceptance tests, we need to distil *what should be done* from the discussion and not really focus on *how* it is going to work. This is a very subtle distinction, but one that is crucial for effective agile acceptance testing.

For example, consider this test script:

1. A new customer registers
2. The customer places three books in the shopping cart
3. The customer goes to check-out
4. The customer fills in a UK delivery address
5. The system offers free delivery to the customer

The script describes how something is tested. But it is not really clear what exactly is being tested here. A fairly good guess would be that this script verifies rules for free delivery, but what are those rules? Is free delivery offered for the first order to the new users? Or is it offered when people buy more than two books at the same time? Maybe it is offered to the customers from the UK? Or is it a combination of those three things? Maybe this example does not describe free delivery rules at all, maybe it demonstrates the general flow of activities in our online store. Now compare the script to the following statement:

- Free delivery is offered to UK customers when they place their first order

This is the same example, restated better and focused on the really important pieces of information. It is much shorter and easier to understand. It does not leave so much space for misunderstanding. If a developer was given the first test as a target for implementation, he might focus on something completely irrelevant such as the number of books in the cart. In the case of the second test, the situation is completely clear.

Adding more examples to the story, such as another order for the same customer from the UK, or first orders of customers from the US or France, will only make the first test script harder and harder to understand. The second test stays fairly easy to comprehend:

- Free delivery is offered to customers from the UK when they place their first order
- Free delivery is not offered to customers from the UK when they place their second order
- Free delivery is offered to customers from France when they place their first order
- Free delivery is not offered to customers from the US when they place their first order

This example is a bit simplistic and the difference between these two approaches is often much greater on real projects. Test scripts spanning a few pages might be easily summarised in a sentence or two without losing any of the important details. Instead of having to read and understand dozens of pages, developers and testers can focus on a paragraph of text. That makes it much more likely that they will hit the target when they implement or verify the functionality.

A very common symptom of problems is to specify business rules using a workflow, such as in the case of the free delivery rules in the previous example. Workflows in acceptance tests are so often there by mistake that I look at any workflow tests now with serious suspicion. There are genuine workflows, of course, but much more often a series of steps describes how something should be tested rather than what is to be tested.

In addition to making it harder to focus on important issues, test scripts that describe *how* over-constrain the implementation. By specifying how something should be done, these tests don't allow developers to find a better solution for the same problem. If specifications only cover *what* should be done then developers have more freedom to implement good solutions.

Apart from the benefit of clear and efficient communication, distilling specifications from scripts also has significant technical benefits. Acceptance tests written as specifications rather than scripts are much more stable and much easier to maintain in the future. If we need to change this rule and offer free delivery to the first three orders, changing all the related scripts would be laborious and error-prone. It is much easier to modify the specification when everything is focused and listed on the same page. Script tests are more error-prone – if a step in a script changes and it was not really important for the goal of the specification, the test will fail and the whole script will have to be updated and reverified. If the rule was expressed directly, those changes would not affect the test.

Rick Mugridge and Ward Cunningham wrote that many people become disillusioned with automated testing because of the pain of maintaining workflow tests, and that such problems typically signal that business rules are not being expressed directly ([9] p. 133). This is true not just for workflows, but for any test scripts that do not specify rules directly. David Peterson was the first, as far as I know, to point out the difference between scripts and specifications clearly, calling for people to "write specifications, not scripts".[3] This is one of the core ideas behind his acceptance testing tool Concordion.

Distilling the specification from the examples and the discussion during the specification workshop is the key to creating acceptance tests that are a good target for development and testing.

Specifying business workflows

Not all workflows are bad and sometimes scripts are a useful tool as well. With examples that describe true workflows, such as page transitions in a web application or a time-based messaging system,

---

[3]http://www.concordion.org/Technique.html

it makes a lot of sense to describe the example in the form of an English language text or even a diagram.

Formalising workflow acceptance tests in the BDD format given-when-then (see the section *Working with business workflows* on page 57), is a good practice that will help you produce better tests because it limits each test to only one setup-action-check sequence. Such tests are easy to maintain and understand.

In the section *Dealing with processing workflows* on page 54 I touched upon the subject of how to analyse and specify examples for larger workflows, in which steps relate to individual business rules. The main emphasis in the discussion and resulting examples should be on the individual business rules, to avoid the combinatorial explosion of all important cases. However, to make sure the overall workflow is explained and understood, and that the steps are executed in the correct order, it often makes sense to have one or two acceptance tests for the whole larger workflow to verify key paths through the steps.

It is very important not to just take and copy acceptance tests for individual steps and create a monster test that is unreadable and unmaintainable. The goal of these few overall workflow tests is just to specify how parts are connected and verify that they are connected properly. The overall test *should not* be used to specify how individual parts work in all possible cases. Individual acceptance tests or test suites should be written to specify the functionality of individual parts. The workflow process itself will probably be complicated, so don't make it even harder to comprehend by complicating it more with unnecessary details. Just take a really simple case and explain how the system should handle it overall. The test should fit into the given-when-then template, with all the relevant actions in the 'when' part. Resist the urge to verify the results of individual actions. This functionality should already be specified and verified by more focused business rule acceptance tests, so you don't actually need it in the overall flow test.

Converting examples to tests

Formalising examples into tests is also a chance to clean them up and focus on important aspects. Specification workshops are intended to spark informal discussions and allow us to explore different paths and examples. The examples that come out of these discussions often have more details than are required for particular tests.

Each test should specify only one thing

When formalising examples into tests, be careful to identify individual rules and specify a separate test for each of them. When several rules are described in a single test and the first rule changes, this will affect the results and validity of the rest of the test. Maintaining such tests becomes a pain because we need to analyse and rewrite parts that are not related to the particular change and then reverify the tests with business experts. If the same example is formalised into several smaller and focused tests, then only a single test is affected by a single rule change. For example:

1. Mark is a VIP customer. He adds $50 worth of flowers to the shopping cart and goes to checkout. On checkout, he is offered free delivery since he is from the US. He can select free delivery or keep it for the next purchase.

2. Then Mark completes the purchase, and starts again. Now he adds a $40 flower arrangement to the shopping cart and goes to checkout, but he is not offered free delivery since he did not order at least $50 worth of flowers. If he had saved the free delivery voucher for the next purchase, he will still be offered free delivery. If not, he will only be offered normal delivery.

The second step in this example continues the first one, but verifies a different rule. In essence, completing the purchase or the total cost in the first step are not really important for the second step. The only important thing is whether someone has an unused free delivery offer. So we can rewrite this as several independent verifications:

- Mark is a VIP customer. He adds a $50 flower arrangement to the shopping cart and goes to checkout. On checkout, he is offered free delivery since he is from the US.
- Mark is a VIP customer from the US and has a previous unused free delivery offer. He adds a $30 flower arrangement to the shopping cart and goes to checkout. On checkout, he is offered free delivery.
- Mark is a VIP customer and has no previous unused free delivery offers. He adds a $30 flower arrangement to the shopping cart and goes to checkout. On checkout, he is offered regular delivery regardless of whether he is from the US or not.

Trying to specify several things at once is also a common problem with tests described as workflows, so this is one more point to watch out for if you are using scripts rather than specifications.

Converting scripts to specifications

You can often simplify a large number of similar scripts tests into a single simple specification. Watch out for sets of related examples described by similar scripts that differ only in some values in the story. Combine all the examples into a single test that only depends on the changing values and specify the underlying rule directly as a single table of argument values and expected rule outcomes. Cut to the basics and throw out all the things that do not really influence a particular rule. Here is what the test for the three workflows in the previous section would look like:

Customer type	Country of residence	Has unused free delivery offers	Order value	Free delivery offered?
VIP	US	-	50	Yes
VIP	US	Yes	30	Yes
VIP	-	No	30	No

Tests should be self-explanatory

David Peterson suggests[4] that acceptance tests should be self-explanatory with a plain English description of the rule at the top followed by the examples, that examples should only demonstrate the rule and not include any extraneous details, and that they should not be merged into the description. An example of a good acceptance test is shown in Figure 5.1.

Figure 5.1. A good acceptance test

Free delivery

Free delivery is offered to VIP customers once they reach a certain number of books in their cart. Regular customers, and VIP customers beneath this threshold, do not receive free delivery.

Examples

Given the threshold for free delivery is 10 books or more, then we expect the following:

Type of customer	Number of books in cart	Free Delivery?
VIP	8	No
VIP	9	No
VIP	10	Yes
VIP	11	Yes
VIP	12	Yes
Regular	8	No
Regular	9	No
Regular	10	No
Regular	11	No
Regular	12	No
.....		

Focus the test on the rule being tested

A test should have just enough detail to provide a full context for understanding and verification, and no more. If you are demonstrat-

---

[4]in a private e-mail

ing a special bonus rule that is applied to shopping carts with more than 50 products, but the details of these products are irrelevant for the rule, then do not list 50 products by name in the test. Write a single step that will populate the cart with a number of random products, in this case 50. Even in cases when you do want to list all the products, keep the attributes actually being set in the test to a minimum. Leave out everything that is not relevant for a particular test. This will make tests easier to read and easier to maintain. If you later remove an attribute from the product class, you will not have to go through 50 examples and clean them up manually. The more irrelevant information you strip from a test, the longer it will stay valid because change requests and modifications of the parts that were removed from the test will not affect it.

Remember to investigate parameterisation

One possible problem with focusing on real-world examples is that sometimes we lose sight of the big picture. With rules such as the one about 50 products, it is important to discuss with customers how the system will be parameterised and how likely the value is to change in the future. Hard-coding limits and thresholds often makes little sense, so we should describe the rule in a more abstract way but include realistic examples for concrete values. This will allow the system to evolve more easily in the future.

This becomes even more important for applications that support several customers with seemingly different business rules. I do not like the idea of customer-specific acceptance tests, because the customer deployment is often just a particular configuration of the system. I've seen a case where the team activated functionality specific to particular customers by checking configuration parameters linked to the customer name. For example, if we had two customers called Big Sports and Live Betting, parts of the system were activated based on values of configuration parameters IS_BigSports and IS_LiveBet-ting. There are several problems with this approach. First, after a while the second client wanted some of the same functionality as the first client, so the team had to duplicate verifications and complicate the code for these cases. Second, these particular configurations change over time and new clients could sign up who want some functionality from both systems, leading to IS_OurNewClient parameters that are a mix between the previous two. Instead of creating customer-specific functionality, always think about actual parameters, thresholds and switches and then build rules that change depending on these switches. Big Sports and Live Betting configurations should be sets of parameter values rather than parameters themselves. Instead of creating customer-specific acceptance tests, work out how the rules are parameterised and then include realistic examples for different sets of parameter values.

Automating tests

Toyota spearheaded the success of the Japanese motorcar industry, changing the image of Japanese cars from cheap junk to reliable high-quality vehicles. One of the major forces behind this success was their innovative production system, which included a specific attitude towards product quality called *zero quality control*, described by Shigeo Shingo[15]. Zero in this case applies not to 'quality', but to 'quality control'. In the Toyota Production System, quality was something that was created from the start and planned in, not controlled at the end. The point of testing in zero quality control is to ensure that items are produced correctly – to prevent defects, not to discover them at the end. This is how we should look at the tests in agile acceptance testing. They are there to prevent us from doing something wrong in the first place rather than to catch mistakes at the end.

Zero quality control introduced the concept of source tests and mistake-proofing devices. Mistake-proofing devices are used to check whether a part is defective right there on the production line. A key feature of these verifications is that they are inexpensive, so that parts can be inspected frequently. A worker can verify a part on the manufacturing line, then it can be verified again before assembly and again later in the process. In knowledge-based work, such as software development, time really is money. The biggest cost on software projects is often related to the time people spend on different tasks. Acceptance tests are our mistake-proofing devices. In order for them to be effective, we have to be able to execute them frequently and quickly, without taking too much time from developers, analysts, testers or anyone else. The best way to achieve this is to automate as many tests as possible. Having acceptance tests in an automated form allows us to easily check whether the code is on the right track as often as we want.

There are lots of test automation tools available today, and your choice of automation tools will dictate how the tests are written, what you can automate and how to automate them. I discuss some of the more popular tools for automating agile acceptance tests in Chapter 10. In this chapter, I focus more on the general constraints of automated acceptance tests. If you are browsing through this book and not reading pages in sequence, you might also want to read an argument against automation in the section *Adopting in phases* on page 151 after reading this chapter.

Keep tests human-readable

The examples that we are turning into acceptance tests are, first and foremost, communication devices. We use them to build a shared understanding of the domain, but then they become a live record of how the system should behave, and ultimately how the system does behave once it has been implemented. When formalising examples into tests, we must take great care to keep them in a form that is easily understood and can be used as a basis for later discussion, especially if we need to get them signed off by a senior stakeholder. For acceptance tests to be effective, they have to be automated but also have to be human readable. And 'human' in this case also includes those who cannot decrypt the Matrix code on the fly.

If you choose to use an automation tool that makes tests understandable only to programmers, then you will have to maintain the test set in some other shape such as a Word document. Maintaining two separate forms of the same thing can cause consistency problems, and violates one of the basic rules of good software development –

don't repeat yourself. This is why I really prefer using tools that allow us to write acceptance tests so that business users can understand them.

Every automation tool has its own way of specifying and automating tests, so programmers need to translate the examples chosen for tests into code or some form of scripting. As I've mentioned before, translation often causes problems because things get lost or become less precise. Ideally, we want to avoid translation as much as we can. Some automation tools allow us to write the description of a test separately from the code automation part. When using tools like this, it is possible to skip the translation from examples into tests altogether. For example, the test in Figure 5.2 could be automated with FIT.

Figure 5.2. A FIT acceptance test

Discount Offers

Frequent buyers are eligible for a discretionary discount. Orders over a threshold should be sent for review to a trader, who may apply a discount.

For a threshold of	20	here are the examples
previous orders this year		next order eligible for discount?
10		No
30		Yes
19		No
20		Yes

The automation part of this test may post actual orders or just update a field in the database that says how many orders a customer has had this year, depending on the design and implementation of the system. But at this point we really don't care about how something will be implemented, just what it should do and why. By focusing on the description of the test, not on the actual implementation or inner workings of the system, we can zoom in on the important things. For example, a question I'd raise is: does a threshold of twenty mean that the twentieth order is eligible for a discount or does the rule apply from the twenty-first order?

This separation also helps to promote specifications over scripting. The test description can focus just on the specification and not on how the actual test steps will be implemented. The test automation part can hide the complexity of scripting.

The tool that you choose will drive the format of the test, so you should ideally try to write examples in a format that the tool can directly understand or be very close to this format, so that the chances of introducing problems during later test automation is minimised. This also removes the need to maintain two separate records of the same tests.

Automating examples with unanswered questions

Specification workshops sometimes end with unanswered questions. Luckily, this does not prevent us from starting to automate the examples. Lots of acceptance testing tools split tests into two parts: the description and the automation. The description structure dictates what the system should do, the automation part describes how the test is executed, but individual values in the description do not influence the automation.

For example, if the test description contains 'John has 50 chips in his account', the automation code stays the same even if the user is not called John or if he has more money at his disposal. The automation part for the discount eligibility example in Figure 5.2 won't change even if the customers change their minds about the case with 19 previous orders.

This division is done primarily to keep the test description human-readable and shield business people from any code implementation details. If you use a tool that separates test descriptions and test automation, programmers can start automating tests even if some questions are still unanswered and the tests contain some unconfirmed results. The structure of the tests will most likely not change, even if the values do. This often gives developers enough to start with, and they can tweak the underlying automation a bit later to accommodate structure changes if required.

What do we do with things that cannot be automated?

With any set of examples, it is likely that some of them just cannot be easily automated. As a general rule, try to automate as much as you can, but do not be overzealous. Some scenarios with lots of external dependencies can take so long to automate in a development environment that it is simply more economic to give these examples a manual run several times during development.

Performance and scalability constraints and expectations are a typical example. A thorough stress and load test of an enterprise web system typically requires distributed deployment on production-quality hardware and enterprise-class storage for the database. Development teams rarely have such hardware at their disposal during development. Usability expectations also fall into the category of things that cannot really be automated. Usability is a subjective quality and requires assessment by people. Usability testing also requires observers with relevant knowledge and experience, not readily available on most software development teams I've worked with.

Just because something cannot be automated easily does not mean that the ideas and practices described in the previous two chapters do not apply. If the user interface is important for the success of the project, then we should use the specification workshop to discuss examples of user interfaces and make sure that they are consistent with business rule examples. Non-functional requirements and specifications such as performance and scalability should also be discussed, so that the implementation team is aware of these expectations and the members understand the constraints and reasons behind them. Acceptance tests can be formalised for these cases as well, although not automated, so that we know what our targets are. Then we can verify these targets several times during the project and make sure that the end result is fit for purpose.

This also applies to important user interface expectations and examples. In almost all my talks about FIT and FitNesse, someone from the audience points out that user interfaces cannot be described with these tools and that their team is used to focusing on wireframes and UI examples. You do not have to be constrained to a single tool. If a user interface example is so important that it should be automated and verified frequently, then use a different tool such as Selenium or one of the other UI robots. Regardless of whether you automate them or not, discuss important UI examples during the specification workshop, in terms of both wireframes and workflows, so that everyone understands what is expected.

Dealing with user interfaces

User interface tests can be a very effective tool if used properly, but misusing them can cause a lot of pain and is a common source of problems in agile acceptance testing.

Don't describe business rules through the user interface

Customers are used to thinking about the system from the point of view of a user of the front-end interface, so they often offer examples in the form of user interface workflows even though they actually want to demonstrate a business rule.

Describing business rules in the terms of the user interface is generally not a good idea because such descriptions will be scripts, not specifications. UI scripts are often too explicit and it is hard to get through the workflow and user interface constraints to the business rules. A lot of clicking, selecting and dragging may be required for a simple variable assignment in domain code. Testing a business rule properly through the user interface may require many very similar tests, with only minor workflow differences. For example, testing the free delivery rules in the section *Distilling the specifications* on page 78 through the user interface would typically require registering a user through the web site, logging in, adding products to the shopping cart and then going to checkout, then verifying web page contents.

With current tools, user interface tests run too slowly to be executed often, making them a lot less effective as a guide for development. User interfaces also tend to change a lot, at least on the projects that I am involved in, so tests that involve a user interface are brittle and the effort to maintain them in the long term often negates the benefits of automation.

Many acceptance testing tools can connect directly to the business domain layer of software and automate tests at this point, allowing us to avoid user interface constraints and workflows and execute tests much more quickly. Business service tests are much easier to manage because they can be executed in a transaction and just rolled back at the end, making it very simple to clean up after tests and ensuring that tests are instantly repeatable. User interface tests do not give that luxury. You can speed up user interface tests with dedicated hardware and grid computing solutions, but they are still still a lot more expensive (in terms of time and hardware used) than quick tests executed directly against a domain layer on the developer machine.

For all these reasons, as a general rule of thumb, *avoid describing business rules with user interfaces.*

Domain-specific languages for user interface tests

Mickey Phoenix presented a very interesting session called *Domain-Specific Testing Languages*[5] at the Agile 2008 conference in Toronto in August 2008. His basic idea was that acceptance tests should be done through the user interface, otherwise they will require a lot of trust from the business people, since users are not really able to see and confirm the effects of tests below the user interface. A green bar from a business-domain layer test tool is not the same as a web screen popping up with the correct information. The first requires a level of trust that the system is really doing what the test says, but the second one makes it obvious.

Mickey Phoenix suggested creating a small domain-specific testing language to describe user interface concepts and steps. This language is then implemented in a general-purpose programming language and connected to a user interface automation tool. So, for example, a simple verification such as 'user is disabled' might actually be implemented as several calls and verifications across the user interface. This implementation of a domain action would analyse web page elements to verify the business functionality and hide all the gory details of HTML form submission and any additional workflow required to navigate to the appropriate page and check whether a user is actually disabled. Having a small domain-specific language definitely helps to make user interface tests more understandable and usable as a guide for development. This approach is similar to xUseCase recorders, which provide record-and-replay automation for thick client applications but allow testers or developers to name recorded actions and use them to build larger scripts (see the section *TextTest* on page 183 for more information).

This idea does have some appeal, but I believe it is still much better to avoid user interfaces when describing business rules at the moment, at least for the kind of projects that I am involved with. If the

---

[5]http://www.solutionsiq.com/agile2008/agile-2008-domain.php

complexity of a system is in the business domain, it makes much more sense to automate tests at the business service level. Again, don't take these ideas as something carved in stone – your projects might require a different approach if the main complexity of the system is in the user interface.

Although I do not agree with Mickey Phoenix's focus on user interface tests, I am mentioning his ideas here because the concept of testing through the user interface to make the effects obvious without requiring any level of trust or abstraction from the customers is certainly appealing. A major obstacle to this idea is poor tool support, but agile acceptance testing is an emerging practice and we do not have all the answers yet. As I explained in the introduction, poor tool support is one of the biggest problems generally at the moment, and I expect much better tools to appear soon. Perhaps someone will come up with a much better web testing tool that would allow us to execute user interface tests faster and write and maintain them more easily and so make this idea more practical.

Specifying user interface workflows

If you want to apply the ideas of agile acceptance testing and specification by example to complex user interfaces, make sure that you focus the tests only on the things that really sit in the presentation layer. Workflow and session constraints are good examples of this. For example, a user interface test might verify that the shopping cart summary is presented first, then the delivery options, then the order confirmation screen. Leave the details of delivery options offered to clients for a business rule test.

Tools such as Selenium (see the section *Selenium* on page 187) allow us to automate browser actions and implement user interface tests. As I mentioned in the section *Distilling the specifications* on page 78, describing a test using low-level workflow steps and actions is not the best idea, so you might want to abstract it a bit and make the tests easier to understand and maintain.

Simon Stewart suggests using the *Page Object*[6] pattern to make user interface tests easier to maintain. In this approach, we describe web pages and the logical operations they support with Java objects and a fluent interface, hiding the complexity and details of user interface commands in their methods. Tests are then written against the page objects, not directly against the APIs of the test automation tool. This approach makes it possible to write tests before the user interface is ready, because we can work with page objects and logical methods that will later be connected to a web site. It also means that tests are less affected by user interface changes, since we only need to change the page object when a particular page changes. Page objects are essentially another version of the domain-specific testing language idea, but in this case the 'domain' is the workflow of a particular web site that we are building.

Who should write acceptance tests?

In more traditional processes, a business analyst is typically responsible for writing specifications and communicating with clients, so a business analyst is a logical candidate to identify the examples in conjunction with the customers and write the acceptance tests based on them. Developers have to automate the tests and connect them to the code, so some companies charge the developers with writing tests and then communicating them back to the analysts. A third choice is to get testers to write acceptance tests, which is in a linguistic sense logical.

All these approaches are, in my opinion, wrong. If developers write tests, then they often turn out to be too technical and action-oriented. If the business analysts or testers write them, then they often have to be changed so that they can be automated. A better solution is to write the tests collaboratively.

The specification workshop is a good time for developers to influence the way that examples are written down and reorganise them straight

---

[6]http://code.google.com/p/webdriver/wiki/PageObjects

away so that they can be automated and connected to the code more easily. For example, if FIT or FitNesse is used as the automation tool, a developer should think about fixture types that can be used to automate test steps and may suggest rewriting some parts to make the automation easier. Customers, business analysts and testers are there as a safety net to prevent developers from going too far and making the tests too technical.

If you do assign a single person to write the tests, make sure that you know what you are doing and why you are doing it. This person is put into a position of significant power and responsibility, as acceptance tests are the specification of the system. If you would not trust someone to write the specifications, don't trust them with writing acceptance tests either.

I heard about a case where the task of writing acceptance tests was assigned to a junior external tester, just because he had some previous exposure to FitNesse. A specification workshop was not held. A developer with no previous experience of writing FIT fixtures was told to automate and review the tests. These two guys just wanted to get the job done, so they wrote the tests the best way they could, making up the content themselves. I have a hard time imagining a worse way to write acceptance tests. Without any domain knowledge or understanding of the problems and requirements, they had absolutely no chance of capturing the real rules and constraints. They made up their own theoretical examples, so the chances of identifying any functional gaps were very thin. Introducing agile acceptance testing in this way can only lead to disappointment, because all the additional work will bring absolutely no benefits. Acceptance tests written by people who do not understand the business and don't have any influence on the scope are completely useless and your team is actually much better off without them – programmers will at least not receive wrong specifications.

If a single person is charged with writing the tests, this person must understand that her job is to research realistic examples and interview domain experts on expected behaviour, not to make up theoretical examples and definitely (and this is of crucial importance) not to provide the answers herself. The job is probably suited best to a business analyst, but she must communicate the tests to the rest of the team and ask for feedback on examples and suggestions for interesting edge cases from developers and testers. Unless such cases are identified upfront, development will suffer when functional gaps are identified later in the process.

Donald Gause and Gerald Weinberg suggest that a technical review meeting is the main tool that ensures that traditional requirements contain all and only reliable information ([3] Ch. 20). Organising a technical review of acceptance tests is probably a good idea if a single person writes them, but an even better idea would be to write the tests collaboratively during a workshop. The workshop can serve as a review meeting as well. Gause and Weinberg also suggest scrutinising the final list of their black-box requirements tests (which relate to acceptance tests in our case) with a team that includes members of the implementation team and professional writers ([3] p. 258). The review should be specifically focused on looking for over-constrained descriptions that might impede good design and then revising them to give more freedom for designing the solution. The professional writers are there to improve the clarity of the specifications written down as acceptance tests. I have never tried to do this myself, but it might be an interesting idea to try out if you have professional writers available.

What acceptance tests are not

A set of acceptance tests replaces the requirements and specifications of traditional processes, but it is not used in the same way. I want to point out some very important differences for those of you who modify the process I describe here to suit your organisation.

They are not set in stone

Workshops do a good job of flushing out inconsistencies, but the acceptance tests for a live software system are never complete and final simply because the software is not complete – it changes with the client's business environment. Collaboration during specification workshops leads to a much more complete set of examples, but some functional gaps and ambiguities usually get through to the development phase. I've done no scientific research to give you exact figures, but from my experience workshops produce significantly more complete and accurate specifications then a single person in a traditional process. Working with realistic examples makes people think harder, so they are less likely to change their mind.

This means that, with agile acceptance testing in place, there will be far fewer changes than with a traditional process, but we have to permit changes to happen to achieve complete customer satisfaction. A large majority of changes after workshops are typically driven by business people changing their minds ('I thought about the thing that we had on the whiteboard yesterday, and I actually think that it should be like this...' or 'I talked to Steve about the edge case, he does not agree'). Tests are a live specification of the system and they can change after workshops. Don't just take the approved set and hold on to it as if it was set in stone.

They are not handover material

There should be no handover of specifications from business analysts to developers. If someone needs to own the tests because of the organisational culture, then the business people should own them throughout the project. Developers should not be able to change tests without telling anyone. The job of business analysts is not complete when the tests are printed and signed off. Tests serve as a focus for development and to facilitate future changes of software, which again require the active involvement of business people. I cover these topics in the next two chapters.

They are not mechanical test scripts

Tests are executable specifications, but executable here refers to a potential to be executed, not to a primary goal of tests. One of the most common problems with acceptance tests is to put too much emphasis on execution. All members of the implementation team are prone to this tendency. Developers sometimes go too far with making tests easier to maintain and execute, making them very technical and not understandable to testers or business people. Business people and testers, on the other hand, are fond of using copy and paste operations. Once they understand how a tool works and they have a good example for a partial specification, they are quite capable of producing very detailed and precise descriptions spanning hundreds of rows or columns in a table or incredibly complex flow scripts. This is often a result of trying to make things very precise and not thinking of examples as something that will be read later.

It is easy to fall into this trap if any single person is charged with writing and maintaining acceptance tests, because different roles have different concerns about tests and benefit from them in different ways. Many testers, especially if they come from a record-and-replay testing background, don't really care about the inner details of a test script, they mostly worry about the result being green when it completes. Business people want to describe the system as precisely as they can, using a template that developers understand. Developers want a detailed specification, but they frown on duplication and having to maintain hard code to integrate acceptance tests. This is why acceptance tests should ideally be owned by the whole team.

This does not mean that complex tests that cover a full range of different permutations are not worth writing, just that they should not be included in the basic acceptance test suite. Nothing is preventing you from creating an automated test that verifies hundreds of permutations and checking the specification of this test with your customers. Such a test can be a very useful functional regression testing tool but it is not a good choice for an acceptance test.

The weird thing about this and the problems described in the previous two sections is that where the problems exist, acceptance tests can still be functionally correct and executable, we can still run them and get a green or red result, but they are absolutely useless as a communication device. So they miss the main goal – facilitating communication. Remember that acceptance tests only work when you can use them for discussion. If a test page becomes too complicated, think about describing the same test from a higher level of abstraction or break it down into pieces that are easier to comprehend.

They are not a complete verification of the system

I have seen people get overly enthusiastic about acceptance testing and start to rely on them completely for testing. This does not work and always leads to disappointment in the end. Automated acceptance tests are a very powerful tool, but they are not a silver bullet. They do not and should not replace exploratory tests through the user interface. Most acceptance tests execute against business domain services, not through the user interface, so small problems in workflow and UI layers can creep in even if all acceptance tests are passing. These issues might be small and easy to fix, but a lot of them can render the system unusable from the user's perspective and be very embarrassing. Such issues can only be discovered with a human actually looking at the user interface, not with automated acceptance tests. Automated acceptance tests do help in the sense that they leave us with much more time for exploratory testing, since they assure us that the underlying business logic is working correctly.

The primary role of acceptance tests is to facilitate the transfer of knowledge and help us build a shared understanding of what the system should do. They are not a quality assurance tool, even though they can help with QA.

Stuff to remember

- Select a set of representative examples to be the acceptance criteria for the next phase of the project.
- Clean up and formalise these examples as acceptance tests.
- Write tests collaboratively, ideally at the end of the workshop.

- Write the examples in the workshop in a form close to what your automation tool can understand.
- Each test should specify a single business rule and be focused only on this rule.
- Keep tests in a form that is human-readable.
- Examples should demonstrate the rule only and not include any extraneous details
- Acceptance tests should be self-explanatory with a plain English description of the rule at the top followed by the examples
- Prefer specification over scripting. Describe *what*, not *how*.
- Acceptance tests are the specification. If you need to get a sign-off, get a sign-off on them.
- Acceptance tests guide development.
- Acceptance tests are used to prevent defects, not to discover them.
- Automate acceptance tests to make them easier to verify.
- Not automating everything is OK.
- Using more than one tool for automation is OK.
- Avoid describing business rules in terms of the user interface.
- People can add and change tests if they find functional gaps or if a domain expert changes his mind.
- Acceptance tests should not be handed over. They remain in the joint ownership of the team.
- Acceptance tests only work when we can use them for discussion.
- Acceptance tests are not a complete verification of the system.

Chapter 6
Focusing development

With traditional abstract requirements, many details are often left to developers to work out. Although business analysts would probably not agree with me at this point, from the perspective of a developer who was typically charged with the task of digesting 500-page documents and then working out what actually needed to be implemented, I can assure you that this is true. Agile acceptance testing helps a lot in this respect, because it gives us acceptance tests that were collaboratively produced to tell developers exactly what is needed. Once the acceptance criteria for the next phase of the project are captured in acceptance tests, the expected result of development is clearly specified in a measurable and verifiable form. From this moment, the actual development can focus on fulfilling these requirements.

A short note before we continue: although I generally try to keep this book non-technical, this particular chapter may be a bit too technical for business people because it deals with the actual implementation process. Feel free to skip it if you are not a developer or skip over parts that seem uninteresting.

Building software to satisfy acceptance tests

Acceptance tests should be considered the specification for development. *They should be an authoritative and reliable source of what the software should do functionally*, and developers can use them as targets to implement pieces of code. Other artefacts such as functional design documents, requirements lists and any other kind of specifications can be produced if they help people think or communicate better, but the functionality specified in acceptance tests is what ultimately counts.

One of the ideas of agile acceptance testing is to flush out inconsistencies and functional gaps before the development of a feature starts. The specification workshops facilitate this. As a result, developers should have much less trouble completing their tasks than with more traditional specifications and requirements documents. When they start working on a particular service or domain object, most of the requirements and descriptions of the expected behaviour should already be specified in the form of realistic examples. This is the ideal and sometimes things will need to change later and some functional gaps will be identified during development, but this happens significantly less often than with traditional specifications. In practice, acceptance tests provide a very good specification for all the required functionality and a solid foundation for development. For a piece of code to be considered complete, everything specified in relevant acceptance tests should be implemented and confirmed by running the tests. Mike Scott wrote[1] that in his organisation acceptance tests are used to measure the progress of development, in a metric called *running tested features*. In his opinion "any other measure does not contribute to delivering value to the business".

Looking at this same idea from a different perspective, the specification is complete also in a sense that if something is not there, it should not be implemented. The code should implement what the acceptance tests expect – no less and no more. Focusing the development just on the things expected by acceptance tests helps a great deal to prevent just-in-case code from leaking into the system. Ben Rady suggested this rule of thumb for acceptance test coverage:[2]

> *And if you've got code that's not covered by acceptance tests, you need to ask yourself this question: Can I delete this code without affecting the functionality of the product? If so, you should...simpler is better. If not, then you should probably write some acceptance tests if you want to ensure that:*
>
> *1. The customers are clear about what the system does.*

---

[1] in a private e-mail
[2] http://tech.groups.yahoo.com/group/testdrivendevelopment/message/24125

2. The system continues to do it.

Developers often focus too much on the technical capabilities of the system and put in extra features that they suspect will be useful in the future. Mary and Tom Poppendieck argue that this might seem harmless, but it is in fact a serious waste ([16] Ch. 1.) Code implemented just in case it is needed still has to be maintained, compiled, tested and managed. Without clear needs and requirements from the customers, this code may become obsolete before it is actually used, or it may never be used. Having the code in the system leads to more complexity and provides one more possible point of failure. The Poppendiecks suggest a prescription to fight this complexity as: "write less code"[21].

Suggesting new features

This does not mean that developers cannot think of new interesting features. However, instead of deciding on their own that a feature is useful and adding it just in case, developers should suggest the feature during a specification workshop. This is the place and time to discuss such ideas. Then the workshop participants can accept the idea and work out a representative example of it, or reject the idea and throw it out of the scope. This also ties in with the discussion in the section *Communicating intent* on page 29, especially the anti-goals or list of things that we do not want to do.

The list of examples that are chosen for the formal set of tests at the end of the workshop should be complete in the sense that it should cover all the required differences in possibilities, so if something is not on the list we do not need it in this phase of development. As you get more accustomed to acceptance testing, ideas about features will be flushed out more and more during the workshop and not during development.

Some functional gaps or ideas might be identified later in the process, especially when you are starting with agile acceptance testing. In this case, developers should grab a business person and discuss the idea during the iteration. If the change is small and you have enough time to include it in the current iteration, you can just add to the examples and do it. If the customer representative or a business analyst is not readily available, or the change is too big to include it in the current iteration, it is better to leave the discussion for the next workshop. In any case, you should try to understand together why this example was not spotted during the workshop and try to make sure you identify all the examples next time. This discussion can take place during the iteration retrospective.

It is also important to remember that acceptance tests are not dead or set in stone. They are very much alive and subject to change. Developers may notice that they need to clean up details or require more information to complete the task or the clients may come up with some more requirements or change their minds. Small changes to acceptance tests should be allowed during development, provided that they are communicated to everyone involved. It is not uncommon for a test to be taken out or another test to be introduced during the implementation. This is perfectly fine as long as everyone understands what the changes affect. If you want to introduce a large change, think about organising a mini-workshop to discuss the change with other team members or waiting for the workshop scheduled for the next iteration so that you can make sure that everyone understands the change.

Designing software based on acceptance tests

Test-driven design is a buzzword often connected with unit testing and lately with agile acceptance testing. With lots of different definitions of this buzzword, people sometimes take it at face value and expect the software design to somehow magically evolve from unit or acceptance tests. In my view, this is a wrong expectation and it will lead to major disappointment. Good software architecture and design do not appear out of the blue sky. Acceptance tests are specifications, not design documents. They are a view of the system from the customer's perspective and as such they should not imply software design.

Agile acceptance testing is not a design technique, just as it is not a development methodology. You can theoretically use any software design practice with acceptance tests, although in practice it only works with techniques that support incremental and iterative design. The way that workshops build up specifications in small stages makes it very hard to do a precise global system design at the start of a project. Building specifications with acceptance tests phase by phase allows us to incorporate knowledge from previous phases of a project, which leads to the improvement and refinement of the system design and architecture.

From my experience, the best results are achieved when there is an overall architectural vision formed at the beginning of the project and then the design is built up incrementally in accordance with the vision. Note that the word 'vision' does not imply detailed specifications or something set in stone, but an idea that is simple and clear enough so that people can relate to it and use it as a guideline. Software should be designed just-in-time as new components in the system and simplified and refined iteratively to be consistent with the overall vision.

Acceptance tests provide design hints

Having said all that, acceptance tests can provide very useful hints about the interfaces between business services and domain objects. This is where the idea of test-driven design comes from.

For example, an acceptance test that specifies required payment details can hint at the structure of our domain object for a credit card. From the test in Figure 6.1, we can suppose that our card will need a type, card number, cvv code, issue number, and start and expiration dates. The test also suggests that the domain object or a related business service will have a method to check card validity.

Figure 6.1. A test suggests domain object properties

card type	number	cvv	issue	start date	exp. date	valid
mastercard	5111111111111111	123			09/12	yes
mastercard	5222222222222222	123				no
maestro	5333333333333333	123		09/07	09/12	yes
switch	5444444444444444	123		09/07	09/12	no
switch	5555555555555555	123	1		09/12	yes

Similarly, a workflow test could suggest business service methods and their arguments:

- *Given* that Mark places 50 chips on number 12
- *and* Tom places 10 chips on number 13
- *When* the roulette wheel spins and stops on Odd
- *Then* Mark loses
- *and* Tom wins 20 chips

This workflow test hints that the service would most likely have a method to place chips on the table, with a player, amount and selected field as arguments. It also hints that there should be a method to spin the roulette and a method to check how much a player won.

Just make sure not to take these hints as design requirements. For example, it would be false to assume from the fact that the acceptance test specifies the roulette table field Odd that the Spin() method for the roulette business service takes the result field as an argument. Code using the roulette table should not be able to specify the outcome of the game, but we need exactly this in a test. The link between the test specification and the business code for this step would have to be implemented using a test system instead of a real random number generator, for example, but not through the business service.

Tests should be focused on the behaviour under test and they often do not provide the full precise context. For example, if a special bonus should be applied to shopping carts with more than 50 products, the acceptance test for this should specify a case where the cart has 50 products (as described in the section *Focus the test on the rule being tested* on page 84). It would be wrong to assume that this implies a business method which randomly generates a number of products to fulfil the test workflow. On the other hand, this test hints at the need to count the products in the cart, which should most likely be implemented as a domain method.

Design does not have to be feature-driven

If these ideas sound similar to feature-driven design, don't take them as implying that you have to adopt feature-driven design in order to use acceptance testing. I want to stress again that agile acceptance testing has nothing to say about the way you design the software. Other design techniques are all viable options as long as they can work in an iterative fashion. Domain (model)-driven design in particular is a very good fit for iterative processes. With domain-driven design, you might want to explore several examples that will be developed in future at a less detailed level, in order to achieve deeper insight into the domain. Agile acceptance testing does not stop you from doing this. It does not help in any particular way, but it does not prevent you either.

You can look at the stories for the whole delivery milestone and discuss some of them with the business experts in order to get enough information to build and verify your model design. These examples should not be put into acceptance tests at the start – they can be included later when the time actually comes to develop them. You might want to capture them in order to kick-start a later specification workshop, but you do not have to do this.

Evolving the design

One more important idea to mention about software design is the practice of using tests as a sort of scaffolding to hold the software together during architectural clean-up or redesign. Refactoring is a term coined by Martin Fowler to describe improving the design of code without modifying the functionality. This practice depends on automated tests to notify us if we change the functionality during redesign and clean-up, so that we can quickly spot and correct any problems introduced. The idea is often summarised as 'red-green-refactor'. The phrase describes a typical development cycle. We should first write tests to specify what we are going to develop. These tests will initially fail ('red') because there is no code to satisfy them. Then we write the code to make the tests pass ('green'). After this, we clean up the design and improve the fit between the new code and the rest of the system ('refactor'). Running the tests again allows us to ensure that we did not break anything during the clean-up.

The 'red-green-refactor' idea is often mentioned in the context of unit tests, but it is actually better suited to acceptance tests. Acceptance tests describe the functionality from the perspective of customers, without going into technical implementation details. This customer view of the functionality is really what must not change before and after refactoring. Unit tests specify and later reflect a particular technical design. When the design improves, these unit tests are likely to break. Acceptance tests, on the other hand, should keep running correctly regardless of the changes in the technical design.

Developers should be able to adjust and refine the technical design as long as the functionality that customers observe stays the same. We develop the code to satisfy the acceptance tests, then, once the tests pass, revisit the design and make the new code fit better with the rest of the system. Rerunning the tests ensures that the functionality is still there after the code is cleaned up. This is how the software design can evolve supported by tests.

Developing the glue between code and tests

With automation tools that allow us to split the description of the test from the automation part (see the section *Keep tests human-readable* on page 87), each specification workshop ends when the test descriptions are written down. Developers then implement the domain code and the test automation part in parallel, with glue code to connect them. This glue code allows us to effectively separate the specification from implementation details. Ideally, all scripting details should be encapsulated in the fixtures, leaving the acceptance tests focused purely on the specification (see the section *Distilling the specifications* on page 78).

Because the glue code is a link between domain code and acceptance tests that business people can understand, it often ends up being very ugly from a coding point of view. This sometimes bothers developers because it is contrary to what they are normally expected to do. Changing the glue code often requires changing the test descriptions as well. *If you decide to change test descriptions, make sure that the new descriptions are still easily understandable to business analysts and customers.*

Most tools will allow you to extract common parts of acceptance tests into a set-up or a tear-down section, so that you can reuse them across several tests. Re-organising tests like this to improve reuse is a good thing, because it makes them easier to maintain. However, make sure that you don't go too far. Resist the urge to fix the glue code and refactor tests so that they are aesthetically nice from the coding point of view but require big changes in test descriptions.

I have no perfect solution for this problem. I would only say that while the glue code might be ugly and a bit of a pain to maintain, it provides improved direction during development as part of the agile acceptance testing practice. The trade-off delivers.

Use the project language consistently

It is very important to keep in mind during development that the language used in acceptance tests should be reflected in the code as well. In the section *Building a domain language* on page 66 I explain how the specification workshop helps us establish a common language for the domain. In development, we want to use this same language for the concepts in our code and avoid creating a technical jargon for the project.

Acceptance tests help promote the ubiquitous language concept of domain-driven design, because they give developers an obvious choice of names for domain elements described in the tests. Consistent use of the domain language in examples and tests will lead to a consistent use of the language in code as well.

Concepts in the code should be given the same names as the respective concepts in test descriptions and in other documentation. During the implementation of the tests, you may notice some inconsistencies in naming. This is perfectly normal especially in the early stages of the project, since the language is still being formed and we do not use anything to enforce formal naming conventions during specification workshops. In two different tests we may refer to the customer's address as 'mailing address' and 'home address'. When you start implementing those two tests, you will notice the difference because code compilation enforces formal naming. When things like this are found, developers should communicate with the business people and decide which name to select, and then consistently use this name. This also means adjusting one of the test descriptions to make it consistent with the code.

If you introduce a new domain concept during implementation because it is required to complete an example, but the concept does not appear in the tests, my suggestion is to contact the business people again and ask them to suggest a name for the concept. Don't just give a class the first name that comes to your mind. If the concept is a first-order domain member, the business people may well already have a name for it. Let's use names for our classes and objects that the business people can understand too. This will make it much easier to discuss the concepts.

Unit tests vs acceptance tests

Due to a combination of linguistic confusion and years of training to avoid duplication in code, developers often raise the question of whether and how they should choose between unit tests and acceptance tests. The linguistic confusion exists because of the word 'test'. If you look at acceptance tests as executable specifications, then the question becomes much less confusing. Should we write executable specifications or unit tests? Why choose between them – we need both.

Unit tests and acceptance tests focus on completely different things. Unit tests act as a micro-target for code units and they check whether the code is correct from a technical perspective. Unit tests should examine edge cases such as empty strings, incorrect formats and various combinations of input arguments that the programmer is concerned about. Acceptance tests act as a macro-target for development of whole code modules and they verify that the product is correct from a business perspective. They examine realistic business cases that the customers and business people are concerned about. Andy Dassing wrote that the unit tests 'will insure the code is built right', and that acceptance tests 'insure the right code is built'.[3]

When acceptance tests are used in the project, large parts of the production code are covered by these tests. Some people tend to skip unit tests because acceptance tests already check the functionality. Although this practice does save some time, it may make it harder to pinpoint problems later. Failed acceptance tests signal that there is a problem, but do not locate the source as accurately as unit tests do. Acceptance tests also rarely check purely technical edge cases, so unit tests should be written to cover these issues at least. Infrastructure parts of the code, not specifically related to any user story, are also not properly covered by acceptance tests.

---

[3]http://tech.groups.yahoo.com/group/fitnesse/message/10115

For example, an acceptance test for a search system might specify that a user can enter multiple search phrases separated by commas in the same line. Somewhere under the hood, this big search criterion needs to be split into multiple criteria. Splitting the search string should be a responsibility of a distinct code unit which is purely technical. The overall acceptance test is not a particularly good target for development of this code unit. It will give us a green or red result, but it will be difficult to know whether the problem is in the code that splits the string into pieces or the code that executes the search. It will also not give us quick feedback while we develop the functionality, as the search needs to be developed as well in order for the acceptance test to run. In cases like these, I prefer to write a few unit tests for the required string manipulation functionality. These tests will allow me to develop and test the string manipulation code unit in isolation and ensure that the unit is correct before I include it in a wider context. Dividing the code up like this also allows us to split the work. One developer can work on string manipulation, another can work on executing the search. The overall acceptance test verifies that both code units cooperate correctly to give the correct business result at the end.

Unit testing tools are often used to perform integration tests or exhaustive system testing. With acceptance testing in place, such tests can be easily dropped. Having acceptance tests in the project in addition to unit tests can help focus the unit tests on what they really should be checking – code units from the programmers' perspective. Unit tests should not verify large workflows, business rules, connect to a database or require any form of external system set-up or configuration. We can move such verifications from a unit test suite to the acceptance test suite and keep unit tests nice and quick.

Some duplication between unit tests and acceptance tests is not really a problem because it does not introduce a large management overhead, and you should not drop legitimate unit or acceptance tests because the same thing is already verified in the other groups.

To mock or not to mock

In order to isolate unit tests from the rest of the system, it is a common practice to use mock or fake stub objects to simplify dependencies. Programmers sometimes take this practice and extend it to acceptance tests. In my opinion, this is wrong.

I like to execute acceptance tests in an environment as close to the real thing as possible and avoid any mocking. Using mock objects in unit tests is OK because it promotes isolation of code units. Using mock objects in acceptance tests can hide serious integration problems. *When an acceptance test passes, the development should really be done.* If mock objects are extensively used for acceptance tests, then you will quickly lose track of what has really been done and what still needs work.

This is why acceptance tests must connect to a real database, use real services if possible and in general provide us with as much assurance as possible that the thing really does what the customers want. Because of this, acceptance tests often run much slower than unit tests. Mocking external systems that have no real test APIs is unavoidable, such as in the example of a random number generator described in the section *Acceptance tests provide design hints* on page 107. Mock objects are sometimes the best solution to verify time-dependent processes or isolate very slow systems. Although they are sometimes unavoidable, I really think that we should keep mock object usage to a minimum with acceptance tests.

Running acceptance tests

A major difference between unit and acceptance tests is also that for most of the time during development unit tests pass and acceptance tests fail. When all acceptance tests pass, the development is done because this means the requested functionality is in place.

Developers should not necessarily run all acceptance tests before committing every change to a version control system, but they should run all unit tests as we want to catch technical bugs before the code goes into the central repository. For unit tests to be effective, they have to run quickly and execute from the integrated development environment. For acceptance tests, it is much more important that they are easily understandable by business people and that they can verify the system in a state as close as possible to the production system.

Acceptance tests tend to be slower than unit tests, because they connect to real databases and external services. Depending on external dependencies, acceptance tests might not really be executable at all on developer machines. Whereas this would be a huge problem with unit tests, it is relatively fine with acceptance tests.

Even if your acceptance tests can run on developer machines, do not include them in the basic build. They will just slow down the turn-around time for implementing small changes. Unit tests should execute on every change to verify that bugs are not being introduced. This basic test run should not last more than a few seconds, as it has to be done frequently. Developers should run acceptance tests to verify that they have finished with a larger piece of code from a business perspective.

Automated acceptance tests are easy to run, although they typically do not execute quickly (or at least not as quickly as unit tests). Developers should take advantage of this and run them periodically to verify that they are on the right track. A continuous integration system should also run acceptance tests for previous phases of the project overnight as a regression test to verify the system functionality. If you do this, it is a good idea to publish the results somewhere where the business people, project managers and customers can see them. This will allow people to see what progress is being made.

Running manual tests

With acceptance tests that cannot be easily automated, it makes no sense to run them throughout the project, but it also does not help to leave them to the end of it.

Instead of running performance and scalability tests regularly and frequently, we can schedule such tests on rented hardware or in a dedicated test centre several times during the project to ensure that we are on the right track. I was recently involved in the development of a high-throughput transaction processing system. We ran a stress test halfway through the project, once the overall architecture started to take shape and there was enough functionality for the test to be relevant. The results were quite disappointing so we asked for outside help and got a consultant to investigate and help us configure the infrastructure properly. Once this obstacle has been removed and we got a satisfactory throughput, we continued developing and then executed another stress test a few months later to reverify and re-adjust the system according to performance expectations. Although early optimisation is a generally bad practice, I do not like to leave the performance testing to the end. Identifying bottlenecks and re-aligning the system a few times during development is usually much better, because we learn from our mistakes and incorporate the knowledge into further development.

The same applies to other types of tests that cannot easily be auto-mated or cannot run on development hardware, such as security probing and usability testing. Instead of leaving these to the end, it is much better to examine the system several times during the project and incorporate the knowledge into further development to promote continuous improvement.

 ## Stuff to remember

- In practice, acceptance tests provide a very good specification for required functionality.

- A piece of code is complete when all the related acceptance tests run correctly.
- Agile acceptance testing does not require you to use any particular design methodology.
- Acceptance tests might suggest what is required, but they do not imply design.
- Resist the urge to clean up test automation code while making test descriptions unreadable.
- Use the same names for concepts in the code as the names used in acceptance tests.
- Unit tests verify that the code is right, and acceptance tests verify that you have the right code. You need both!
- Acceptance tests should run in an environment as close to the production environment as possible.
- Make sure to periodically run tests that cannot be easily automated or run on development hardware.

Chapter 7
Facilitating change

Once the entire set of acceptance tests for a project phase is green, the development work is almost done. At this point, developers might improve the design of the system with some new insights acquired during the current iteration and re-execute the tests to confirm that the system is still working as it should be. After this, we can continue with the next phase of the project. The role of the set of acceptance tests for the previous phase now changes from that of a target for development to that of a utility that facilitates future change. It becomes a live record of what the system does and a set of regression tests that can be executed to verify that the system still does what it was supposed to do.

A live specification

The executable code is often the only thing that we can really trust in software systems. Other artefacts such as specifications, requirements, even API documentation, quickly get out-of-date and cannot be trusted completely. On the other hand, executable code is unusable as the basis for a discussion with business people. Source code is no better, since business people cannot read it. Even if they could read it, source code has too many details to facilitate an efficient discussion about business rules and features. It is too low-level and it prevents us from seeing the wood for the trees.

An automated acceptance test suite, connected to the executable code, can easily be run to check whether it still reflects reality. We can have the same level of confidence in the automated acceptance tests as we do in the code. This allows us to use the acceptance tests written for previous phases of the project as a good basis for discussion. The representative set of examples, formalised into acceptance tests and connected to the code by test automation, plays the role of a live specification of the system – the authoritative source of what the system does and how it behaves.

This kind of live specification is easily understandable by business people and helps everyone understand the business domain. Rick Mugridge gave a very interesting presentation called *Doubling the value of automated tests*[1] at the Google Test Automation conference in London, on September 7th 2006. In this presentation, Mugridge talked about how acceptance tests helped people understand the business domain. Business analysts worked with testers on writing tests, and started noticing inconsistencies and unclear definitions when they wrote test examples. Tests not only helped guide the development, but also allowed people to clarify the business domain and understand the business rules better. When acceptance examples evolve during the project, duplication is removed, workflow rules are flushed out, and acceptance tests become focused on the business domain and express true business rules. Mugridge says that acceptance tests became a "significant and valuable business resource", helping to educate employees on the business.

Having a live and relevant specification of the system helps new team members to get started and understand the project. It also protects us from the 'bus effect', whereby we lose important knowledge if the only person who knows what the system does gets hit by a bus (or in a more realistic scenario leaves the team for a different job).

Keeping it live

During development, we expect acceptance tests for the current iteration to fail most of the time, since the functionality is not yet there. But once the functionality is implemented, previous tests should always pass. After a phase of development is done, it is of crucial importance to promote related acceptance tests into the suite of regression tests. These tests can be used to verify that the system keeps doing what it is supposed to do.

---

[1]See http://video.google.co.uk/videoplay?docid=-7227306990557696708 and http://www.rimuresearch.com/RickMugridgeGoogleConference.pdf

Running acceptance tests for the current development phase overnight and publishing the results is a nice way of informing everyone of progress, but it's not really mandatory. However, running the regression test suite for previous development phases periodically is a necessity. Tests are automated, they run overnight, so there is virtually zero cost in executing all of them. (Except in a very rare case when the whole suite cannot be executed in one night, so you might need to divide it into batches or prioritise tests.)

If one of the tests fails, it means the system stopped doing something that it is supposed to do and this should raise an alarm. A failing test that was previously running is a clear signal that the code is no longer synchronised with the specification, so one or the other needs to be modified. This may be due to a bug being introduced with new code, or because of a change that conflicts with some of the previously implemented business rules. Unless it is completely obvious that the problem is due to a bug (in which case the code should be fixed straight away), customers have to decide whether the example is obsolete or still valid. If the team has a dedicated business analyst, then it is her job to explore this issue and discuss it with customers and stakeholders.

A very important thing to remember is that *regression tests in doubt should never be disabled.* Developers sometimes disable a test to make the alert temporarily go away, but they rarely remember to go back and re-enable it. Tests should be disabled or dropped from the regression test suite only if the functionality is obsolete. Do not ignore the error signals or disable tests to make the problem go away. Either fix it or get confirmation that the functionality specified by the test is no longer valid. I do not advise waiting for the next specification workshop to sort out these problems – deal with them as soon as you can.

A continuous integration system should run the tests and tell someone if any of the tests fail – this will protect against problems creeping into the system. Automated alerts keep the problems small, since we can catch issues as they appear and solve them, and not allow them to accumulate or grow. Otherwise, you will soon be affected by the broken window syndrome.

Broken window

The *broken window syndrome* was first described in an article on police and neighbourhood safety, written by James Q. Wilson and George Kelling and published in 1982 in Atlantic Monthly.[2] Wilson and Kelling argue that disorder in a community, if left uncorrected, undermines efforts to maintain the neighbourhood. The authors suggest that a single sign of carelessness can cause huge problems later, if not taken care of. "One unrepaired window is a signal that no one cares, so breaking more windows costs nothing" is one of the key ideas in the article. Willson and Keeling give an example of litter accumulating on a pavement and not being cleaned up. "Soon, more litter accumulates. Eventually, people even start leaving bags of trash from take-away restaurants there or breaking into cars."

This article and the broken window syndrome were introduced to the software development community by Andrew Hunt and David Thomas in *The Pragmatic Programmer*[18]. They compared broken windows and accumulating problems to issues in the code. If a piece of code is clean and properly covered with tests, programmers who modify it will most likely try to keep it clean. If it already has a ton of problems, they simply will not care. If problems are left to pile up, people stop caring about the design and just hack the code to get their job done – "breaking more windows costs nothing".

Making sure that previous acceptance tests are always valid is also important from the aspect of keeping the specification relevant. Because all tests are passing correctly, we know that the specification is still live and we can trust it in discussions. The periodic execution

---

[2] See [17] and http://www.theatlantic.com/doc/prem/198203/broken-windows

of tests is like a beep on the heart monitor during medical operations, telling us that the patient is still alive.

Because running tests periodically is so important, it should not be left to anyone to choose whether they are executed or not and we should definitely not rely on any single person pushing the button to do it. Continuous integration servers, such as Cruise Control by ThoughtWorks and TeamCity by JetBrains, automatically compile a project from source code and execute tests to verify that it is correct. When a problem is found, they can alert developers and testers by e-mail or signal problems using a Web console. We should use such a system to alert us about any inconsistencies between the acceptance tests that were previously running correctly and our code. When you put acceptance tests under the control of a continuous integration server, remember that a failure in the regression test suite should break the build, unlike an error in the acceptance test suite for the current phase, which is not really expected to pass until the end of the phase.

Acceptance tests are a good start for the regression suite, but don't take this as a suggestion to stop there. Testers should use other tools and methods for supplemental regression testing as they see fit. I want to make this explicit so that there is no misunderstanding. Agile acceptance testing just gives you a good starting point, because it ensures that the business rules are covered. (Comprehensive regression testing is outside the scope of this book.)

Introducing changes

With a live, relevant specification in the form of acceptance tests that business people can understand, we can introduce changes to the system much more easily. The live specification facilitates discussion about change requests, and we can use existing tests to analyse how the requested modifications would affect system behaviour. Existing examples provide a good framework in which to discuss the changes and make sure that we do not forget important edge cases. When we start changing the existing tests and adding new information to them, having things written down on paper, or in an electronic form, will again help us identify new potentially important cases or functionality gaps (as explained in the section *Identifying important examples* on page 50). These changed tests are then moved from the regression test suite back to the active set of acceptance tests for the current phase of development.

Solving problems

With domain knowledge and understanding shared among team members and a comprehensive acceptance test suite based on realistic examples, the quality of the resulting software is much higher than with more traditional specifications and requirements. This does not mean that you will never get any bugs. Nobody is perfect and unfortunately bugs will still happen.

When a bug is found, the key questions to answer are: 'why was it not caught by the tests in the first place?' and 'which set of tests should have caught it?' This will provide insights for future specification workshops. Mike Scott recommends[3] that we should treat defects as evidence of missing tests. If an existing feature is incorrect, then the case was overlooked by the team so we need to add a new test and ensure that similar cases are covered next time. Another possibility is that the case was specified incorrectly, which means that real domain experts did not participate in the workshop and did not review the tests afterwards. To solve similar problems in the future, we need to identify people who should participate in the workshops or review tests for each part of the system. If the system is not doing something that it should be, then a new feature should be put into the development plan and specified when the time comes for implementation. There is also the possibility that the bug is not a domain problem at all and should have been uncovered by unit tests or integration tests, not by acceptance tests.

---

[3]in a private e-mail

Unless the bug is a complete showstopper and has to be hot-fixed on production as soon as possible, I advise modifying the relevant test or writing a new test to demonstrate the bug first. Then the developer can have a clear target for fixing the bug and run all the tests after the fix to make sure that nothing else was broken in the process. With showstoppers that get fixed, deployed and verified in production, this discussion should happen after the resolution when things calm down. It is important to change the acceptance tests in the light of this new knowledge to prevent the bug from resurfacing in the future!

Once a bug verification test is in the regression test suite, it will be executed every time with the other acceptance tests, making sure that a fixed bug stays fixed.

Keeping the software flexible

At the beginning of development, changes to software are quick and simple. As the code base grows, it becomes harder to modify. A simple change in one area often causes problems in a seemingly unrelated part of the code. Without tests, it soon becomes too hard and expensive to change anything. With tests to signal problems, we can be more confident in the code and change it freely.

Because we are gradually building the regression test suite as we are building the functionality, we always have scaffolding that will hold the code together during changes. This allows us to improve the design more easily and to simplify the code, making sure that new changes fit into the system nicely and that we have incorporated new knowledge correctly. Periodical housekeeping keeps the software flexible by making it easier to maintain and extend later. Running the tests after each change and making sure that they all execute correctly tells us that we have not broken anything and that the system still does what it was supposed to do.

Keeping the specification flexible

Although tests might start focused and simple, they usually degrade over time. People will often try to minimise changes to tests when code gets changed or when business rules change, so it is likely that additions and changes will only be made with time. Surplus items that do not really affect the outcome will often not be deleted. Although new insights and breakthroughs in the design of the domain or code changes might uncover ways to write acceptance tests simpler than they were done originally, tests are often kept in the original form if they still work. These tendencies mean that tests will gradually lose their usefulness as a true, live specification, if some effort is not put in to improve them.

Acceptance tests should facilitate change, not impede it. If you find yourself in the position of resisting changing the system because it will take a long time to fix all the tests, then the tests have to be simplified and made easier to change too. This is why, like code, acceptance tests need periodic housekeeping and clean-up so that they remain flexible.

Common symptoms of problems

Here are some things to watch out. Try to avoid them when changing tests, or clean up tests if you notice any of these problems:

- Long tests, especially those that check several rules
- Parameters of calculation tests that always have the same value
- Similar tests with minor differences
- Tests that reflect the way code was written or tests that mimic code
- Tests that fail intermittently even though you haven't changed the code
- Parts of tests or even complete tests used as set-up for other tests
- Interdependent tests.

Long tests, especially those that check several rules

If a test is unusually long, it is often a signal that the test contains much more detail than what is really needed to test a specific business rule or feature. As the system evolves, a long test will be affected by code changes much more frequently than required, since changes in any of the details featured in the test will require you to update it.

Another possibility is that the test verifies several constraints or business rules in a single workflow. In this second case, the test will be affected by changes in any of the business rules and these changes will have a domino effect. If the third step of the test has to be changed, the fourth and fifth will probably have to be updated as well. If the test had been focused on a single business rule, then changes to related rules would not have affected it.

A similar problem can occur with a test that describes a state machine or a calculation with a large number of parameters. This often ends up as a table with a large number of columns. Most likely some of these parameters do not really affect the calculation or the state. They might have been important earlier but became obsolete, or maybe they were just copied from a similar test, but never really affected the behaviour specified by the test.

Acceptance tests can become too long because a number of small changes or related verifications are bolted onto existing tests, as it is easier to do this than create a completely new test. You might make several changes to the test as the code is refined before you spot that it actually describes two or three different things.

In any of these cases, you should look for ways to make the test shorter and simpler. If it specifies several business rules, split it into smaller and more focused tests (see the section *Each test should specify only one thing* on page 82). If it contains extra parameters that are not important for this particular test, delete them. If it is too technical or detailed, try to specify the test from a higher level of abstraction. In particular, move any implementation or scripting details from the actual acceptance test description to the automation code. An acceptance test should ideally specify what the system does, not how it is implemented (see the section *Distilling the specifications* on page 78).

Parameters of calculation tests that always have the same value

When a parameter in a description of a state machine or a calculation rule always has the same value (or keeps the same value in a majority of cases), this is typically a signal that the parameter is not really important for the feature described in the test. If the value is there just because the underlying business method under test needs that argument, then the test automation code can generate a random value or pass a hard-coded value, allowing us to drop the parameter from the test description. This can also happen if the argument was once relevant for the calculation but the rules changed, making it obsolete. Surplus parameters and repetitive code make it harder to maintain a test.

If the value is really important for the calculation, it can be set globally. For example, instead of a table that verifies tax calculation on products with 50 rows with only two types of products mentioned in these 50 rows, we can split the test into two tests of 25 rows, each with a globally specified product type, and remove the product type column from the tables.

Similar tests with minor differences

Lots of similar or related tests with only minor differences are typically a symptom of a business rule explained through scripts rather than directly. Tests such as these demonstrate *how* the underlying business logic works, rather than *what* it is supposed to do. Having different cases for a single business rule broken down into several scripts with just minor differences will make it harder to see the big picture and identify additional important edge cases. This set of tests will be a problem for maintenance because the tests most likely include some steps that are not necessarily relevant for the thing being described. Changes in these seemingly unrelated steps will affect all the tests as well.

This might happen because we started with a single story and then added similar stories as change requests came in. Alternatively, the stories might have initially started off as different but become similar after code refactoring or test clean-ups.

In general, a good solution for this is to convert all the script-style tests to a single focused specification test. This test should only contain the relevant arguments and specify *what* the underlying functionality does rather than explain *how* it works. You can see an example in the section *Distilling the specifications* on page 78.

Tests that reflect the way code was written or tests that mimic code

Acceptance tests should be focused on the customers' view of the system. When tests are too action-oriented or mimic code, they get cluttered with too much detail and make it hard to see the big picture. In addition, they will need to change when the implementation changes even if the underlying business functionality does not.

Tests like these often get written by programmers. Sometimes they are written after the code to increase the code test coverage. This is very dangerous because it is a sign that programmers are changing the specification of the system to match their view, which might not necessarily be the same as the view of the business people. In addition, such tests are often biased towards the implementation. If there is a problem in the implementation, the test hides it and makes it seem as if the system is correct. Any tests written just to increase the code test coverage should be reviewed by domain experts. Tests that are too technical and action-oriented should be rewritten to use a greater level of abstraction.

This does not mean that tests with a low level of detail focused on implementation should not be written. But these tests should be in the set of (programmer) unit tests and not in (business) acceptance tests. As a general rule of thumb, developers should not be writing acceptance tests themselves. Acceptance tests have to be specified collaboratively with business people and testers.

Tests that fail intermittently even though you haven't changed the code

Acceptance tests (and unit tests for that matter) have to be reliable. If they pass, we must know that the system works. Once they get promoted to the regression test suite and fail, there had better be an error or we are going to waste a lot of time investigating for nothing. Once the problem has been found and fixed, we need to be able to trust that a green test is a sign that the job is done. Tests that fail intermittently without underlying code changes are misleading and unreliable – we are better off without them.

Tests that sometimes pass and sometimes fail are a huge warning signal. How do we know that the same thing is not going to happen in production? Many causes of unreliability in tests, such as timing issues, dependencies on database contents and reliance on random values, can be fixed. If the issue is caused by an asynchronous process, we can focus on testing the synchronous parts in isolation for acceptance and then just have a simple overall test to check connectivity. If tests depend on database contents or constraints, they should be wrapped in transactions which are rolled back after the test.[4] Tests that depend on random values might need to be rewritten, or the random value generator might need to be abstracted to make tests easier to write (this is a rare exception where a test mock is useful in acceptance testing – see the section *To mock or not to mock* on page 115).

Regardless of what the cause is, tests like these have to be investigated and fixed, otherwise they will undermine the reliability of regression tests in the future. As a consequence, these tests also undermine confidence in the code under test.

---

[4]http://gojko.net/2008/01/22/spring-rollback/

Tests that fail intermittently might also point to larger problems in the code or the infrastructure that it uses, such as unpredictable background processes or unreliable external resources. In order to prevent these problems from showing up in production, we may need to redesign the system to make it more reliable. For example, instead of directly sending requests to an unreliable external system, we might batch up requests in a queue and make sure that they arrive at their destination. As a nice side-effect of this redesign, the system will become easier to test as well.

Parts of tests or even complete tests used as set-up for other tests

It is not at all unusual to define an example as an extension or continuation of a previous example. Sometimes it's a special case, sometimes it's an alternative workflow. People often create tests for such examples by copying a part of the previous test, or the whole test, and using it as a set-up for the new test case. This has to be done with care because it is the number one cause of bloated tests with lots of irrelevant information. More often than not, we do not need all the details of the previous test case in the new one, especially if the whole test with the trigger and verification is just copied and extended. The new test will suffer from all the same problems described in the section about long tests.

A much better solution is to copy only the details that are really needed, or to extract the preparation phase into a common set-up for the old and the new test.

Interdependent tests

Tests that depend on the order of execution are just a special case of the previous problem – though this is not as visually obvious as in the previous case – and they suffer from the same problems. If a test requires some other test to be executed beforehand to prepare the data or initialise some external dependencies, then a change in the first test might cause the second to start failing with no obvious reason.

In addition to this, we will never be able to execute just the dependent test on its own ever, and complex dependencies like this quickly get out of hand. We need to run individual tests and get quick feedback, not run the entire test suite every time.

Cleaning up tests

Acceptance tests have to be maintained throughout the software life-cycle. Knowledge gained during development often provides new insight into the domain and helps to implement, explain or define things better. This knowledge should be incorporated into existing tests in the following iterations. Here are a few tips for housekeeping that you can apply to keep tests flexible and easy to change.

- Extract interdependencies into a common set-up
- Focus each test on a single business constraint or rule
- Strip tests to basics
- Convert scripts to specifications
- Evolve the language consistently
- Organise tests so that they are easy to find.

Extract interdependencies into a common set-up

Tests should be independent. Every test must be able to be run on its own. This does not mean that we have to introduce a lot of duplication into the tests. Automation tools often provide a way to specify a common set-up and tear-down phase for a set of tests and this is how test dependencies should be resolved. This will allow us to execute tests independently or together and still change common items at a single place when we need to.

Focus each test on a single business rule

Make sure that every test checks one and only one business constraint or business rule. When the functionality changes, we will have to update only a single test and we will know exactly what we are updating. This practice also helps us pinpoint problems when a test starts failing.

Strip tests to basics

Clean up tests by removing anything that is not directly related to the thing described in the test. This will make tests easier to read and understand. Test stripped to basics are also much more stable, because they depend only on the minimal set of domain elements. Changes in other parts of the system will not affect them.

Reducing complexity is also important because we don't want to have to test our tests. Acceptance tests should be easy to comprehend and verify. If they get to the point where it is no longer obvious what the example in the test specifies, then the test loses value as a communication device. I have stressed this several times in the book but I'll do it again: *the real value of acceptance tests is in communication.* This is not to say that more complex test scenarios should not be written or executed, but they do not belong in the acceptance testing suite. An example of this would be a script that verifies integration with a third-party credit card processor by running a set of a dozen cases with each of the fifty test credit card numbers. Such a test script could be described by a table with ten columns (input arguments and expected outcome) and hundreds of rows (different combinations of arguments). This is a very useful integration or regression test, but it is not easy to read or communicate, so it is far from ideal as an integration test. From the perspective of describing what the system does, the same could be specified with a much smaller and more focused test script that is easier to understand.

Convert scripts to specifications

If you notice a number of similar tests, this is most likely a sign that you are missing an important abstraction or trying to describe *how* the system does something instead of directly specifying *what* it does. A common symptom of this is describing business rules through a series of workflows. Look for the underlying rules, constraints and decisions in the group of similar tests and replace all of them by a single specification focused on the underlying functionality. Start by identifying parameters and values that change in the tests. From them identify those that are really important for the goal of the test and remove the others to make the specification more focused. See the section *Distilling the specifications* on page 78 and the section *Keep tests human-readable* on page 87 for more details.

Evolve the language consistently

If you rename classes and objects in code, make sure to propagate the changes to the acceptance tests. Refactoring can make the code language slowly drift away from the test language, creating ambiguity and confusion later on. There must be no technical and business jargon on the project, only the project's ubiquitous language.

Some test automation tools allow you to bind the test descriptions directly to your domain objects, making it easier to spot language inconsistencies since tests will start failing after a change on only one side. In any case, a change in the domain language should be agreed and communicated to everyone involved – developers should not be changing the language on their own.

Organise tests so that they are easy to find

Because acceptance tests are primarily a communication device, it must be relatively easy to locate a particular example and similar or related examples. Almost all acceptance testing tools today allow us to categorise and organise tests into hierarchies and group related tests. There is no universal solution or strategy for this and you should work out what makes most sense for your team and environment, but I want to stress that tests that are not efficiently organised quickly get out of hand.

One way to categorise tests is by iteration, user stories in an iteration and tasks for a particular story. Another is by application module, business rule and then variants of the rule. The first strategy makes more sense for tests in development, as it groups together the target of an iteration while people are working on it. The second strategy makes more sense for long-term test archiving, because it makes it easy to identify and locate tests by business functionality or area of influence. The best approach is to use the first strategy for tests as specifications in development and the second strategy for tests as a record of the system (and regression suite) after development. This means you need to reorganise tests after the iteration ends.

Some acceptance testing tools allow you to set up links in the hierarchy, so that the same test appears effectively in two places but you need to update it only once. With a tool like this, you can actually have both strategies for test organisation in parallel.

Keep tests in a version control system

Acceptance tests define what the code should do and explain what the current code does. They should live (and die) next to the related code. This specifically means that acceptance tests should be kept in the same version control system with the same version organisation as the domain code. A good feature of most acceptance testing tools today is that they store tests in a plain text or HTML format, which works really nicely with source code control systems.

Even if the tool that you choose for acceptance testing allows you to keep the tests separately from the code, resist this urge. It might not be very intuitive, but storing acceptance tests separately from the code will cause huge consistency problems when new versions are introduced or existing code branches are merged. Remember that acceptance tests are a live specification. If you keep the specification and the implementation separate, they will evolve separately. It will not be easy to determine which version of the code relates to the specification, or how to verify a particular version or branch of the code. When the code and the tests are kept in the same version structure, under the same version control system, then the connection between the two is obvious.

Keeping tests in the same version structure as the code also helps if you need to resurrect parts of the system that were modified or deleted by mistake. Recovering both the specification and the implementation at the same time is then easy, as is verifying that they are still consistent.

Stuff to remember

- Acceptance tests are an authoritative description of what the system does.
- We can have the same level of confidence in acceptance tests as in executable code.
- We can use existing acceptance tests to discuss future changes.
- Once the functionality is implemented, previous tests should always pass.
- If an earlier test fails, immediately discuss with customers whether it specifies obsolete functionality. If yes, take it out. If not, you found a bug.
- Regression tests in doubt should never be disabled.
- Automate periodic execution of regression tests using a continuous integration tool.
- Acceptance tests should not be the complete regression testing suite. They are only a good start.
- If you find yourself resisting changing code in order not to have to fix tests, you need to simplify the tests and make them easier to maintain.
- Efficient organisation of tests is crucial to keeping them easy to maintain.
- Keep tests in the same version control repository as domain code.

Watch out for these problems:

- Long tests, especially those that check several rules
- Parameters of calculation tests that always have the same value
- Similar tests with minor differences

- Tests that reflect the way code was written or tests that mimic code
- Tests that fail intermittently even though you haven't changed the code
- Parts of tests or even complete tests used as set-up for other tests
- Interdependent tests

Part III. Implementing agile acceptance testing

In this part, we take a look at some more practical aspects of agile acceptance testing, how it fits into the wider project plan and individual iterations and how to implement it in an organisation. I also briefly present the most popular test automation and management tools and suggest what you can expect from them in the future.

Chapter 8
Starting with agile acceptance testing

Agile acceptance testing is, primarily, a communication and collaboration technique. It introduces a big change in the way that the members of a software project talk to each other, transfer knowledge, specify and document their project. I believe that starting to use agile acceptance testing is more an organisational change than a technical change. It affects the traditional roles and responsibilities of developers, business analysts and testers. The tools and technologies that they use are of much less importance for the change than the way teams are organised.

Agile acceptance testing in the context of the development process

Agile acceptance testing is not a development methodology. It tells us *what* we need to deliver, not *how* to actually develop and deliver software or how to plan the project. Every now and then someone tries to sell the idea of acceptance test-driven development methodology on the Internet, but I really do not buy into this. In fact, there are so many of these X-driven-Y names now that I am really suspicious of anything new that comes in this form. Agile acceptance testing is a communication practice and it helps us build a shared understanding of the domain. The acceptance criteria constititute a target for development, but they do not prescribe how to actually develop the system.

Jim Shore gave one of the best summaries of agile acceptance testing in the wider development context in his article *How I use FIT.*[1] He called the process 'describe-demonstrate-develop'.

1. The first step in the process, *describe*, requires us to say what we are going to develop using a short description, no longer than a paragraph of text.

2. The second step, *demonstrate*, asks us to show various differences in possibilities with examples and captures the actual specification for the work.

3. The third step, *develop*, is the implementation of the specification using regular development practices and methodologies.

4. The fourth step, although it does not appear in the name of the process, is *repeat*. Each pass through the describe-demonstrate-develop cycle should elaborate one small business rule. A project might consist of hundreds or thousands of such cycles.

Agile acceptance testing has much more to say about what happens before development than during it. John von Neumann, the father of modern computing, said: "There is no sense being exact about something if you don't even know what you're talking about". The first two steps make sure that we know what we are talking about before the real development starts.

From a theoretical perspective, the approach of using realistic examples for discussion and learning about the domain and then selecting a set of them as acceptance tests works with any development system or methodology. In practice, however, the approach works best in the context of agile development methods (hence the word agile in the name). I have not tried it in a project that uses the water-fall-style method and honestly I have no intention of trying it in that environment, but my gut feeling is that it would not work so well there. Agile methods break up the project into small time-boxed iterations. Each iteration aims to implement a relatively small, easily manageable piece of the total project scope. Specification workshops to discuss the next two weeks or month of development can be held

---

[1] http://jamesshore.com/Blog/How-I-Use-Fit.html

efficiently, often in one afternoon or a working day. This means that workshop participants do not spend too much time away from their normal duties, so it is much easier to get stakeholders to participate. The small amount of scope means also that the set of tests that come out of the workshop are relatively easily and quickly reviewed, if sign-off is necessary.

With development methodologies that require specifying and discussing large amounts of scope up front, these workshops would last for much longer. Holding up so many people for so long at a time would probably not be feasible. Instead of decision makers and domain experts we would get junior representatives whose time is less valuable. The quality of their feedback would be much lower than the insight of senior domain specialists. With an agile development method, instead of one huge workshop that lasts a month we can have thirty one-day workshops during the project. Getting domain experts away from their daily duties for a day or an afternoon at a time is much easier than getting them for a month.

Agile development methodologies allow us to adjust and change requirements and specifications on the fly, which means that if someone discovers a gap in functionality, we can just easily add another test without really upsetting anyone (as long as they are told that the specification has changed). Having this flexibility is very important, especially when the team is learning how to use agile acceptance testing, since the cost of mistakes in the first two stages of the process is very low and we can allow ourselves to experiment.

The incremental and iterative way of developing also allows us to incorporate the knowledge learned during the project into our examples, specifications and acceptance tests. In the first few work-shops the developers may not know anything about the domain, but by the fifth or sixth workshop they will know quite a lot and be able to contribute a lot more. If we only had one big workshop before the development started, then the feedback that developers bring to the table will not be anywhere near as valuable.

Agile methodologies also do not require a lot of paperwork, so you can build up the specification on the fly using examples from agile acceptance testing. Acceptance tests are the specification of the system. As we add acceptance tests and evolve existing ones, we build and refine the specification. This saves a lot of time and effort because you do not have to produce and maintain large requirements and specifications documents. In fact, having both these documents and acceptance tests might introduce confusion if they are not perfectly in sync. This benefit is obviously lost with methodologies that require sign-off on formal plans and documents (although, as suggested in Chapter 5, you can get sign-off against sets of acceptance tests).

This does not mean that you cannot use agile acceptance testing if you are not agile by the book. People are often scared when too many buzzwords arrive together, so for those of you that are thinking about migrating to agile, I'd like to point out that you do not have to eat the whole elephant at once (or ever finish that meal). Doing unit testing or pair programming or any other popular agile practice is not a prerequisite for agile acceptance testing, and you definitely do not have to learn all these ideas and apply them at once. Agile programming techniques certainly help, not because agile acceptance testing somehow specially depends on them, but because they are generally useful practices. An iterative development model is, however, a prerequisite for effective agile acceptance testing.

Fitting into iterations

The idea of specification workshops that support acceptance testing seems to cause a lot of confusion and even misunderstanding. In many public talks I give about agile acceptance testing, I get questions from people who somehow contrast it to iterative development and mistake the workshop for a big design session upfront, expecting that it will lengthen the feedback loop. Agile acceptance testing does not say anything about how to develop software or organise iterations. There is nothing stopping us from fitting it into an iteration. In fact, it works best with short iterations. Short iterations force us to keep the stories discussed in the workshop short, enabling us to keep the workshop short and focused.

Here is an example of how the specification workshops (and acceptance testing) fit into an agile process to shorten the feedback loop and improve iterative development. The diagram in Figure 8.1 is a version of the iteration workflow that Andy Hatoum and I came up with while I was writing this book. Take this as just a guideline, not as something that you must follow exactly. Hopefully it will make it easier to understand how to apply these ideas in different environments. The contents of the brackets indicate the iteration that a step relates to: N is the current iteration, N-1 is the previous one and N+1 is the next.

Figure 8.1. A suggestion for iteration workflow

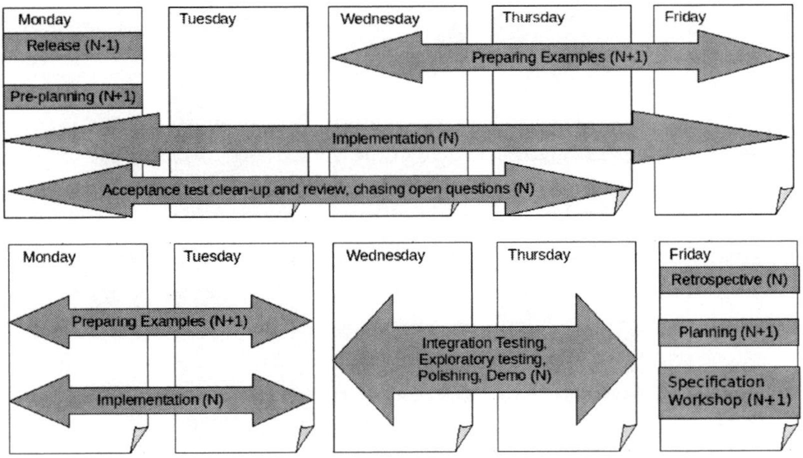

Release (N-1): If we wish to, we can release the result of a previous iteration on Monday. Not every iteration has to be shipped to customers, but we like to have the code as a potentially shippable software package at any point. We don't release on Fridays to reduce the risk of causing production problems over weekends while people are not readily available to fix issues.

Implementation (N): On Monday the implementation of the current iteration starts. This includes all normal agile development practices such as unit testing and continuous integration. An important change for teams already practising agile development is that the development *is focused on implementing acceptance tests specified for the iteration.* Implementation includes running and cleaning up acceptance tests, identifying and discussing missing cases, writing more tests for these cases or modifying existing tests. It also includes releasing to the QA environment often, so that on-site customers and testers can use the software and provide quick feedback. Implementation continues until Wednesday of the second week.

Pre-planning (N+1): The clients, the business analyst, the project manager and the development team leader work out roughly what will go into the next iteration (not the current one, but the one after). This is intentionally a rough plan, not carved in stone, but good enough to give the business analyst and the customers a starting point for discussion and allow them to keep one step ahead. This happens on Monday as well.

Acceptance test clean-up and review (N): Not all acceptance tests that we have prepared for this iteration will be perfect straight away, so a business analyst chases open questions and gets remote domain specialists to review the tests, while the project manager can get any sort of sign-off required for tests, and testers, developers or business analysts simplify, clean up and organise acceptance tests. We expect this activity to span the first few days of an iteration. Changes might be introduced into the acceptance tests later, but we expect the bulk of the work to be done in the first few days and for the tests to stabilise after this. The diagram shows that this should end by Thursday, but this is not a fixed deadline, it is an estimate. Clean-up ends when it ends, sometimes it may not be needed at all, sometimes it will end sooner, sometimes it will spill over to the next week.

Preparing examples (N+1): Once the bulk of the acceptance test clean-up for the current iteration is done, the business analyst can start working with the clients and the testers on the examples for the next iteration, preparing a good starting point for the workshop. The deadline for this is again an estimate. In general, after the work on the current iteration is done, the business analyst should focus on the next one and stay on it until the polishing on release N starts. The important thing is that the examples don't need to be absolutely complete at this point. The goal is to get started and prepare for the workshop, not to iron out all the acceptance tests. This is explained in more detail in the section *Keeping one step ahead* on page 61.

Integration testing, Exploratory testing, Polishing and Demo (N): The development work should be done by Tuesday in the second week of the iteration. At this point, we start polishing the result. The developers will already have been releasing builds to the internal QA environment during implementation, as soon as there was something for others to see. This allows the on-site client and testers to check what developers are doing during the development and provide feedback, but these intermediate releases do not necessarily need to be production quality. However, at this point in the cycle we start to really focus on producing a clean, polished package. This involves cleaning up database scripts, packages, configuration, upgrades from the previous version and testing the installation. Everyone switches from adding new features into exploratory testing and cleaning up the results. Issues, UI bugs and ideas for small improvements get resolved during Wednesday and Thursday. By Thursday afternoon, we should have a polished version that we can demonstrate to off-site customers remotely. Polishing may spill over on to Friday, but this should be an exception rather than a rule.

Retrospective (N): This is a normal retrospective, normally looking at the last two weeks of development but occasionally a longer period. Everyone is involved.

Specification workshop (N+1): We select stories for the next iteration and then nail down the specifications during the workshop by discussing relevant examples. The business analyst introduces the examples that she has prepared with the customers, then we all go through them. The other workshop participants ask questions and suggest edge cases and new examples for discussion. Developers need to think about how they will implement the stories and identify functional gaps and inconsistencies. Testers need to think about breaking the system and suggest important testing cases for discussion. We can organise feedback exercises during the workshop to check whether we all understand the same thing. The aim of the workshop is to build a shared understanding among developers, business people and testers about the aims for the next two weeks of work. Because realistic examples are discussed and written down, inconsistencies and gaps should be easy to identify and we should get a solid foundation for development. The workshop ends when everyone involved agrees that there are enough examples and that everything is clear enough to start the work. Some questions may remain open, because they require the approval of a more senior stakeholder or the opinion of a particular domain expert, but in general the workshop should define the precise scope of the next two weeks' work and ensure that we all agree on this. A representative set of examples is chosen to be an acceptance criterion, and formalised into acceptance tests.

Planning (N+1): Once everyone knows what the potential scope is, we organise estimations, play planning poker and confirm the final scope for the next iteration. This becomes the official plan. Everyone is involved.

After this, we start over with the next iteration.

Igniting the spark

Introducing agile acceptance testing in an organisation by decree and without real buy-in from the people affected will only meet with resistance and cause the attempt to fail. I think that a much better way to introduce agile acceptance testing in an organisation is to start out small and then let this spark ignite a larger change.

The best thing, in my opinion, is to try out agile acceptance testing with a team of people enthusiastic about the experiment on a mid-size project or a module of a larger project. Small projects do not have the communication challenges that would demonstrate the advantages of agile acceptance testing and they are too short for best practices to evolve. A mid-size project can be completed with a relatively small team so you should have no problem finding enough enthusiastic people to try out agile acceptance testing, yet the team will be large enough to demonstrate how agile acceptance testing as a practice helps to improve communication and collaboration. In an organisation with traditional roles, you probably need one business analyst, a few testers and a few developers on the team. It is important for this initial team to be composed of enthusiastic people because they will look for ways to overcome difficulties and adjust general ideas to their environment, rather than just abandoning the new practice and falling back to the usual way of working at the first sign of trouble. Have no doubt, this kind of organisational change will face obstacles on the way. Although most people get into agile acceptance testing within a few weeks, it might take a few months for the ideas to fully settle down and the full benefits of the practice to show.

Once this project starts delivering, the ideas will simply spread virally through the organisation. Boosted by fresh ideas on how to improve communication and collaboration, business analysts will start talking to other business analysts, testers with other testers and developers with other developers in your organisation, spreading the word. Management will notice that there is something different about this particular project because suddenly there are fewer problems in development. People from other teams will phone you to ask how this testing thing works.

As with any agile software practice, nothing should be taken as carved in stone and the initial team members should work out the best ways of applying the ideas of agile acceptance testing in their own environment. These can then serve as much better guidelines for rolling out the practice on a larger scale than the general ideas. You can then swap the people on the original team with some people on other teams and use them as trainers for a larger roll-out.

Don't mention testing

Developers are often enthusiastic about agile acceptance testing. Testers typically sit on the fence, with testing managers sometimes openly fighting against it because they fear that someone is trespassing on their territory. But it's business analysts in a corporate environment who often put up the greatest resistance to agile acceptance testing.

If you want to introduce the practice in a corporate environment with strictly defined roles, avoid using the word testing at all. 'Testing' in the name of the practice often causes a lot of confusion and resistance. Talk about executable specifications or communicating with examples instead of acceptance tests. (See the section *Better names* on page 38 for more ideas.) I've used this approach to deal with business analysts who object to the whole practice because they 'don't do tests' and with testing managers that object to someone else testing the software.

You can organise a specification workshop and formalise the examples that will be used as a specification without ever mentioning that they will be used for testing. Ask business analysts to be there to help programmers work with a new experimental way of building the development specification. Ask testers to be there to provide additional feedback and to learn about the domain. Ask developers to participate to flush out inconsistencies from requirements before the development starts. Then just convert the specifications to tests without involving anyone who might object to the whole concept of automating acceptance tests for development. You can include people who genuinely want to help, be they testers, developers or business analysts, but the rest of the world does not necessarily need to know that you are doing anything related to testing. This is not an ideal situation, but it will be good enough to start with. Make sure to verify the tests with business people once they are written down, again avoiding mentioning the word 'test'. Just ask whether you have written down the meeting minutes correctly. When the time comes to discuss the ideas again, instead of the original Word document, show people FitNesse or whatever tool you are using and just tell them that this is how you decided to store the specifications. When the time comes to test, offer testers a set of already automated verifications for some of the test cases and work with them to define the rest.

After a while, the benefits of this practice should become obvious and then you should be able to tell everyone the full story and start using the name 'acceptance tests'.

Adopting in phases

Brian Marick wrote an article called *An alternative to business-facing TDD*[2] in March 2008, challenging the effectiveness of automation for acceptance tests. Arguing that test automation by itself does not help clarify the design, that live demonstrations can show continuous progress and that automated acceptance tests cannot detect user interface bugs, he concluded that test automation for business facing (acceptance) tests does not pay off as much for code-oriented (unit) tests. He suggested that it might be more effective not to convert the examples into automated tests and perform exploratory testing for acceptance:

> *An application built with programmer TDD, whiteboard-style and example-heavy business-facing design, exploratory testing of its visible workings, and some small set of automated whole-system sanity tests will be cheaper to develop and no worse in quality than one that differs in having minimal exploratory testing, done through the GUI, plus a full set of business-facing TDD tests derived from the example-heavy design.*

Although I do not completely agree with this hypothesis, I think that it is important to include it because Brian Marick is one of the top authorities on testing in agile projects and definitely has much more experience with acceptance testing than I do. His article is relatively short and is a very good read, so if you are sitting near a computer, put this book down and take five minutes to go through it now. If

---

[2]http://www.exampler.com/blog/2008/03/23/an-alternative-to-business-facing-tdd/

you are not close to a computer, make sure you remember to read it later.

I agree that automated acceptance testing can never replace exploratory testing for finding UI bugs and identifying unforeseen problems, but I do not think that these two practices should be competing against each other. With today's automation tools, user interface testing is still a big pain and I consider that exploratory testing is much more effective for user interfaces than automated testing. On the other hand, I see a lot of value in incrementally building up an automated regression test suite for business rules. Automated acceptance tests not only provide assurance that the software meets the goals, they also serve as a very good safety net during design improvements and changes (see the section *Evolving the design* on page 109). They also leave more time for exploratory testing.

The idea of stopping after the specification workshop is interesting from another aspect. The workshop helps to build a shared understanding of the domain and working with realistic examples helps us get more complete and precise specifications. This is, for me, the biggest benefit of agile acceptance testing at the moment. If you think that introducing the whole practice at once might be too much for your team, start by only doing the workshop and then slowly move into test automation.

Choose a facilitator for the workshops

A very good way of making specifications workshops more effective is to assign a facilitator. The role of the facilitator is to ensure that the workshop is on track and that it does not turn into yet another boring meeting. The facilitator should make sure that everyone is participating, both by stopping people from taking over the workshop and by encouraging (even directly requesting) feedback from silent participants. He or she should set the topic for discussion and have the right to change it when the discussion gets sidetracked, especially watching out for personal bickering and parallel discussions. If a developer or tester is trying to explain why an edge case is important and the other participants are dismissive, the facilitator should help the person formulate the example better. If, however, business people acknowledge and understand the edge case and they still dismiss it, the facilitator should ensure that the discussion returns to the cases that are relevant for this particular phase of the project. The facilitator is also responsible for making sure that people discuss realistic examples at an appropriate level of abstraction and in enough detail, preventing the discussion from digressing into unrealistic contrived examples or implementation specifics, but ensuring that it still provides enough context to build a deep shared understanding.

The best person to be a facilitator is someone who has the right people skills and an overall understanding of the domain, possibly not in full detail. This person should be able to speak both to technical and to business people, and help them find a common language. If the team includes a full-time business analyst, she is probably the best person to facilitate the workshop. The facilitator does not have to be a domain specialist. A ScrumMaster or a team leader might also be a good choice. By team leader, I mean someone with personal leadership skills who spends a lot of time communicating with people, not someone who has the role because of great technical knowledge. A key thing to remember is that instead of translating between business and technology the facilitator must help other workshop participants to find a common language.

Writing about collaborative requirements workshops, Ellen Gottes-diener insists that the workshop needs to be a facilitated meeting, going as far as advising against using a workshop for requirements unless you have a facilitator who is neutral to the outcome ([19] Ch.1). Although the specification workshop can be considered as a kind of requirements workshop, I'm not so sure about this prerequisite of a neutral facilitator. I can see the value of a facilitator when a new team is learning how to apply agile acceptance testing, but I believe that smart people can be self-organising once they know what they should be doing. I have often played the role of a facilitator, but I was very much involved in development and never neutral to the outcome.

Even so these workshops produced good results. A good facilitator does not necessarily need to be neutral to the outcome, but the person should be able to take a neutral point of view or even play the devil's advocate to evaluate and stimulate the discussion.

An alternative to relying on facilitators long-term is to promote the culture of a good fight, where open conflict of opinions is encouraged and respected rather than avoided. Naturally, this good fight concept should be limited to the topic at hand and not diverge into personal insults. My opinion is that a facilitator, although certainly helpful, is not essential if the team knows and honours the rules of the game and the goals of the workshop. While the team is still learning what the workshop should be about and defining the rules, a facilitator can help significantly.

Hire a mentor

It always helps to have someone who has gone through the transition to lead the way, answer questions and train project team members. If you can hire someone like this and get him on the initial team, this will help to establish best practices for acceptance testing in your organisation much more quickly. The mentor can act as a facilitator during workshops, help to choose tools, train people to use them and help automate tests better.

Having someone readily available to answer questions and help with problems will speed up progress, but it might also make the team too reliant on the mentor. The ultimate goal is to empower your initial team to work without external help and then even train other teams in your organisation. I think that an especially effective technique is to have someone to help out for a short period of time, such as a few weeks or a month, and then have them go away and let the team members work on their own for a few weeks. Once the mentor goes away, the team members will have to try harder to solve issues and problems on their own, so they will learn more from these challenges. If you work on shorter iterations, then the mentor should be with the team during the initial few iterations, then leave the team to work out examples and produce tests for one iteration themselves, joining towards the end of it to review the outcome and help them solve any open issues before the specification workshop for the next iteration. As the project progresses, the mentor should join for shorter periods of time and leave for longer, making the team more and more self-reliant. After a few such visits, the mentor can just occasionally visit the team to discuss progress. He can be available for phone or e-mail consultations throughout. A good mentor will pass the knowledge on to the initial team in a few visits, so the entire experiment should not take more than two or three months.

Where to look for a mentor

Agile acceptance testing is an emerging practice and there are no official organisations or professional societies that you can turn to and ask for a mentor. I would be wary of any consultants who try to sell themselves as certified trainers for this practice. This is not to say that someone with a certificate is necessarily a fraud, but look for experience rather than paper qualifications. Your best bet for the role of mentor or trainer would be someone who has already gone through this transition in another company similar to yours, so you could try to snatch someone away from the competition.

Don't look for a mentor in an official organisation – look for a consultant on mailing lists such as Agile Testing (agile-testing), Agile Aliance Functional Testing Tools (aa-ftt) and FitNesse Yahoo groups and the Agile Acceptance Testing group on Google groups (links are in the Resources appendix). My company provides in-house and public training courses for agile acceptance testing. See http://neuri.co.uk for more information on this.

Avoid the cargo cult mentality

In some places, developers try to get acceptance testing introduced from the bottom up by writing acceptance tests themselves, using the requirements documents as a guide, without discussing the tests with business people. This might seem like a good start, but it is actually as wrong as it can possibly be.

Cargo cults

During World War II, Allied forces and Japan invaded isolated islands in the Pacific where the natives had had no contact with the rest of the world before. They arrived with modern equipment, built airfields and delivered supplies by cargo drops. Some of the supplies were shared with natives, drastically changing their way of life. When the war ended, the soldiers and their supplies were gone. Religious cults developed on the islands calling for the cargo to start falling from the sky again. Islanders built elaborate models of airplanes and air control towers out of straw and wood and imitated soldiers, hoping to summon the presents from the gods. Needless to say the presents never arrived.

The term 'cargo cult' was introduced to programming by Steve McConnell, who characterised the ritual following of practices that serve no real purpose as cargo-cult software engineering in 2000.[3] Since then, this name has became synonymous with any blind use of programming practices without really understanding the underlying principles, which often does not bring any benefits.

If developers write acceptance tests based on their understanding of the system, they are not actually checking whether this is the same as the understanding of business people. The result is that people are disappointed because acceptance testing seems not to provide any benefits apart from regression test coverage. If you think about it, since there was no effort to build a shared understanding, there can be no benefits of improved communication. Acceptance tests written in this way are no better than the straw air-control towers and wooden planes that the Micronesian natives built. They follow the outer

---

[3][20] and http://stevemcconnell.com/ieeesoftware/eic10.htm

structure and provide an image of something useful, but the core is missing and the benefits are simply not there.

If developers decide that they want to implement acceptance testing and there is no buy-in from the business experts to organise specification workshops, there can still be some benefits but they will not be as effective as with full cooperation from the business experts. A model that may work is for developers to write tests after the requirements are handed over but before development starts. They can then ask the business people to verify the tests, trying to initiate a discussion during the verification. This approach can be implemented on a small scale, with one or two developers discussing tests with a business analyst or a customer. It will at least allow these people to synchronise their understanding and might be the first step toward introducing the full workshop practice later in the project.

In the introduction, I said that you should use the process described in this book as a guide rather than something carved in stone. You will probably want to modify some parts to make it fit your organisation better, but make sure that you follow the core ideas and underlying principles. Otherwise you will end up following a cargo cult.

 Stuff to remember

- Agile acceptance testing is not a development methodology.
- Iterative development is a prerequisite for effective agile acceptance testing.
- Start out small, with a team of enthusiastic people.
- Think about assigning a facilitator for the initial workshops.
- Don't take practices as carved in stone, adjust them to your needs but keep to the basic principles.
- Avoid mentioning the word test to get the buy-in of people who think that testing is beneath them.
- Developers should not write acceptance tests themselves.

- If you cannot get business buy-in at least to review the tests, don't do acceptance testing – you will just waste time.

Chapter 9
Planning with user stories

In this chapter, we take a look at how agile acceptance testing fits into into a wider project perspective, specifically in the context of user stories. User stories are today the most popular technique for planning agile projects. Although there is nothing peculiar to agile acceptance testing that requires you to plan with user stories, these two techniques complement each other incredibly well and produce the best results when they are used together.

I have intentionally placed this chapter towards the end of the book, because I wanted to emphasise the communication benefits of acceptance testing and avoid focusing too much on general software development practices and techniques. How you plan your project depends very much on the type and size of the project and the period available to you to develop it, so please don't interpret this chapter as something that is carved in stone or prescribed as the only way to do things. You do not have to base your plans on user stories, although there are significant advantages to using them if you are introducing acceptance testing. If you understand the underlying principles and ideas of user stories you will be able to see more easily how to fit agile acceptance testing into your planning process, and you might even find that you can improve it.

This chapter is intentionally short. It will probably leave you with many questions about the practical application of user stories. I want to encourage you to investigate this topic further. The bible for user stories is Mike Cohn's book *User Stories Applied for Software Development*[11]. I strongly recommend reading this book if you have not already done so. For ideas on how to work with user stories more efficiently, also see *Agile Estimating and Planning*[12] by the same author.

User stories in a nutshell

A *user story* is a very brief description of what the system does for its users to help them perform their work more easily. It describes the system from the viewpoint of the user, not from a technical perspective. There are no details of how the system implements the required functionality in a user story, or even what the detailed requirements are. All specifics are left for later discussion. Stories are used to plan out the project broadly, by focusing on customer benefits. Typical stories are fairly high-level, allowing us to discuss plans and prioritise deliverables without getting tied up in implementation details or flushing out all the requirements.

From a more traditional point of view, user stories describe the *scope* of a project, but not the *specification*. At a very high level, they answer *what* and *why*. There are no details because we want to avoid paralysis by analysis, getting lost in the details and not seeing the wood for the trees. Leaving the details for later also allows us to keep the initial scoping discussion short and efficiently use the time of project sponsors and key stake-holders who need to be involved in building a high-level delivery plan and scope.

I like to use one-liners as user stories; any more is probably too much detail. The classic template for user stories is:

1. As a *role*,
2. I want *functionality*,
3. So that *benefit*.

The behaviour-driven development community promotes a different story format, moving the benefit to the first position to emphasise it. The BDD story template is:

1. In order to *benefit*

2. As a *role*

3. I want *functionality*

For me, there is no significant difference between these two formats, but some people religiously insist that one is better than the other, as if a change in the order could really make an important difference for the project. This reminds me of the famous curly brace discussions and similar coding format issues, which were always so pointless but wasted so much time. Ken Arnold's legendary article[1] asking for style wars to stop always comes to my mind in these situations.

How are stories different from more traditional methods?

The most important difference between user stories and more traditional techniques, such as use cases, is that user stories are there to facilitate the discussion and support planning rather than to be an authoritative description of system requirements. Use cases often live on throughout the project as a load of printed material with formal sign-offs, but user stories are just placeholders for discussion and information which will come later. For much more information on the differences between user stories and use cases, see [11] Ch. 12.

The worst case of people not understanding the point of user stories that I have seen was a project plan that included product CRUD (Create, Read, Update, Delete, typical data entry screen capabilities) as a user story. A user story might include product maintenance, but it should also specify for what purpose and by whom the maintenance is performed and it should describe something that will deliver some real business value to the customers. When you understand who needs to create, update and delete products and why, the scope of the story is often a lot less than in a generic case. A generic product CRUD case would typically include everything required for product maintenance in the whole system. A true user story includes only what is needed

---

[1]http://www.artima.com/weblogs/viewpost.jsp?thread=74230

to provide a particular business benefit to a particular user. Some of the fields, relationships and validations do not need to be implemented to fulfil the job of a particular user for a particular story. Even more importantly, some other functionality might be required to complete the story and make it really usable in production. For example, if the products were also presented to customers on a public web site, even if they were not sold in the first iteration, this might bring some business value. If creating and updating products is not enough to bring real business value, then the implementation of a product CRUD story will just sit in the testing system without actually being used.

Benefits of user stories

User stories empower development teams and customers to prioritise and scope projects so that customers get real value for money much faster and the time and effort of everyone involved in project planning is used efficiently.

I do not think that there is any specific benefit to user stories over more traditional planning methods if you want to deliver everything in one big chunk, you are sure that the requirements and the specifications will not change during the project and your developers are domain experts. But most of my projects are not like that. Plans change, requirements are thrown in or out and clients want staged deliveries. Developers often make wrong assumptions about the problem domain and misunderstand requirements and they learn about the domain while developing the software. If your projects are like this, you will find that user stories use your time efficiently, reduce waste and provide a very good framework for discussing, planning and prioritising with key stakeholders. They also help to flush out wrong assumptions and help developers make better decisions.

User stories are lightweight and, as the name suggests, completely focused on the users' point of view. Because of this, customers can easily relate to the stories and have a much better grasp of what the functionality described by a story actually brings. This makes comparing, prioritising and scheduling much easier. Instead of asking the client to decide between implementing an e-mail service or building a graph-optimisation subsystem, we can discuss priorities in terms of something that they can relate to, such as finding the best route for travelling or sending confirmation letters in the customer's chosen language. This is a subtle distinction that can take a while to settle in the mind when you first start to use user stories. The main idea is to plan in terms of business benefits and customer experience, not technical tasks or infrastructure requirements.

Of course, technical and infrastructure constraints may influence planning and they should do so. For example, it might make a lot of sense to implement an accounts system before developing an interface to payment gateways, or to implement support for generic e-mail notifications before providing language-specific e-mail features. Such considerations need to be taken into account, but talking in terms of something that the customers can relate to allows us to plan more efficiently and to get better feedback from them.

With planning methods that focus on technical tasks, functionality gets translated into work items and the plan is built based on these tasks. When the plan changes later or when priorities shift, it is not always easy to see which tasks are required to completely implement some business functionality so that it can be used in production. User stories avoid this problem by skipping the step in the middle. Customer expectations are not translated to technical tasks. Instead, they are used directly in planning, so that things don't get lost in translation. We plan using items that clients can directly relate to, with a clear understanding of how parts of the plan bring business benefits. When business priorities change, user stories provide a really useful framework for discussion and prioritisation. Clients should have no problems deciding which user stories are no longer required, or which ones should be rushed through to implement a key requirement.

Another great feature of user stories is that each story brings a clear immediate customer benefit. If you build your delivery plan with user stories, each deliverable brings direct value to the customer. If the plan is built on a purely technical basis, infrastructure components often take precedence in development, so the customers cannot really start using the software until much later in the project. With a plan based around user stories, it is not uncommon for even the first deliverable to go into production and be used to solve real problems. This builds confidence in the product early, avoids big-bang integrations and enables customers to give us much better feedback. In fact, that's the way I prefer to deliver my projects – I simply don't trust software that is not live.

Three Cs of user stories

Ron Jeffries wrote a famous article on three essential aspects of user stories called *card, conversation,* and *confirmation.*[2] These three aspects later became known as 'the three Cs of user stories'.

- *Card*: User stories should be written on small index cards. The card allows you to write down only so much information, so nobody can mistake it for a complete requirement. The card is just a placeholder for discussion and a tool for planning.
- *Conversation*: the card is used just as a token for discussion, reminding people what to talk about. The conversation is where we flush out all the details and get to real requirements.
- *Confirmation*: each user story should be verifiable, and we should have a clean way of deciding whether it was implemented correctly and completely.

User story cards

Cards can be shuffled around, grouped with other cards and put on the wall, helping us to see the big picture and plan efficiently. Because of this, it makes a lot of sense to put information that helps with planning, such as priorities and estimates, also on the card. A very good idea is to choose a concise story title and put this on the card as well, so that people can easily refer to a particular user story.

---

[2]http://www.xprogramming.com/xpmag/expCardConversationConfirmation.htm

Connextra pioneered the index story card format that is now more or less considered standard. The Connextra story card has the story title and priority at the top, followed by the story description, and then the story author, submission date and implementation estimate at the bottom. An example is shown in Figure 9.1.

Figure 9.1. The Connextra card template

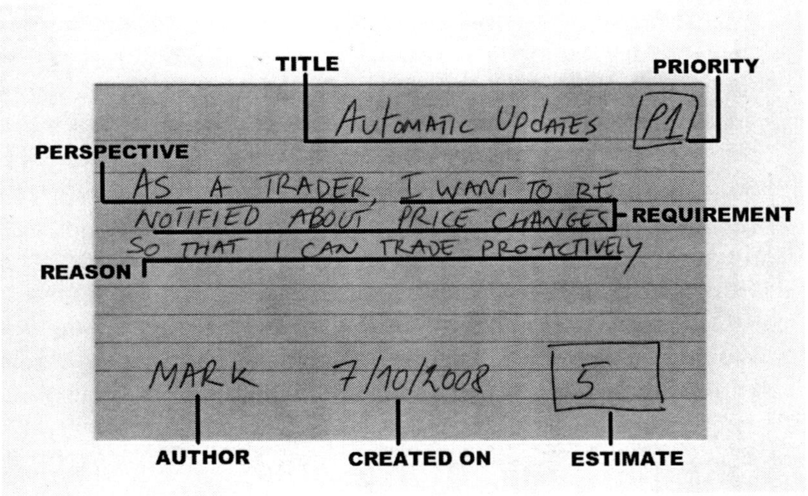

Project planning

I like to use a brainstorming session with key stakeholders at the beginning of a project to create the first cut of user stories, writing them down on index cards or sheets of paper that are then put up on a wall. We first discuss very high-level stories (sometimes called *epics*) and then break them up into smaller stories later. The way that the stories are gathered is not really important for the topic of this book – see the recommended books on user stories for some good techniques for that. What is important is that each story should have something to say about how the system will help users do their job when it is complete, and why this particular functionality is important.

During the brainstorming session, it is not uncommon for people to add some stories that seem to be related to the project, or describe what they would like to have in the long term, but which turn out to be less important as the others. Some stories might even conflict with other stories. Once the first cut of the user stories is captured, key stakeholders need to decide which ones are actually going to make it into the project. Having stories displayed on the wall helps everyone to see how big a particular project is going to be, and the overall picture helps to persuade people to throw out irrelevant stories and focus the development. We can use the vertical grouping of the sheets to signal the benefits or goals of a group of related stories (for example, group all stories that automate transaction processing together), and use an abbreviation or some other indication to specify the user role. So instead of the full description 'As a security investigator, I want the system to automatically identify high-risk transactions so that I do not have to manually analyse them' we just write 'identify high-risk transactions' on the sheet of paper and put it on the wall. This short description later becomes the title for the story. In any case, we should be able to link a sheet of paper on the wall to the user role and know why the story is on the wall in the first place.

Grouping into deliverables

Collected together, all selected user stories make up the scope of the project. Armed with this collection of stories, we can split the project into deliverables that are complete in a sense that they can be used in production. This forms the basis of our release plan, which we can then split into iterations ordered according to priorities. As a rule of thumb, I suggest grouping user stories into deliverables so that each deliverable has a clearly defined business goal target. This allows us to prioritise by focusing on business goals and benefits rather than on technical dependencies. In a recent project for an e-commerce system, we split the fraud detection system into three deliverables:

1. The first deliverable automatically retrieved and consolidated fraud alerts from various sources and opened investigation tickets, saving the investigators a lot of manual work.

2. The second deliverable automated part of the investigation process by automatically blocking the disputed account and notifying external partners that all pending financial operations were to be frozen. This deliverable automated a time-critical part of the investigation, so that potential fraudsters could not do any more damage. The investigators then had more time to look into the actions that had taken place on a disputed account and decide whether it was really a fraud or just a false alert.

3. The third deliverable automated the decision process for obviously fraudulent cases, again saving a lot of time for the investigators and allowing them to focus more on the cases where a human eye was needed.

Focusing each deliverable on a clearly defined business goal makes it is easy to decide whether a story belongs there or not. Each story clearly states why it is required ('... so that'), so it is obvious which business benefits are fulfilled by a story. This is one more benefit of planning with user stories. Focusing on goals means we can identify stories that have no related goals and leave them out, making the project much more coherent and providing grounds for discussions about why something should not be in scope (or at least not yet).

There is more than one way to skin a cat, so you should try reshuffling stories and deliverables a few times looking for the plan that brings customers the most important benefits the fastest and makes sense from a technical perspective. Once everyone is happy with the plan for deliverables, a high-level project plan is more or less already in place – it's on the wall! Although there are no details in the stories, technical experts should be able to give rough estimates for how long the development will take and how many people they need for the project based on the list of stories.

A crucial idea, from a planning perspective, is to build blocks of software that can actually go to production. There are so many reasons for this that I do not know where to start. Project sponsors will be really happy when they actually have something to show to justify the costs of development. Software that saves money or brings in new business has a much better effect than something you can just demonstrate on a testing system. The customers will start getting business benefits early. End-users will start flushing out small problems and identifying unforeseen functional gaps earlier. Programmers will receive much better and much earlier feedback on their work, allowing them to build this knowledge into the later phases of the project. There are many other reasons why iterative development is now preferred to the classic waterfall model, and they all apply here. In essence, we want to go live with software as soon as we can, and then keep delivering chunks that also go live at regular intervals.

A good delivery plan has these features:

1. Each individual deliverable is relatively small so that it can be developed and delivered in at most a few months.
2. Each deliverable can actually go live and it will be useful to users.
3. Deliverables will take about the same time to develop, so that we can release deliverables at similar intervals.
4. The order of development technically makes sense.

I use a simple question as a rule of thumb to decide whether a deliverable is functionally complete: 'Pretend it's magic and we already delivered this piece of software. Would it actually be useful and usable in production?' If the answer is 'No', then we discuss which stories are missing to enable this.

The user stories method does not give you detailed estimates of how much something will cost or how many months it will take to develop. On the other hand, I would argue that even a seemingly precise traditional method based on detailed requirements would just produce an educated guess that would not necessarily be closer to the actual outcome than the suggestion of an experienced team leader. And such detailed methods take a lot more time and effort from key stakeholders, whereas planning with user stories makes sure that their time is used efficiently. Senior stakeholders are often quite busy and working on a number of other projects, so it is really important that they focus on the plan and give real feedback. In my experience, it is much easier to get people's full attention for one afternoon than to chase them around for endless meetings until all the details are flushed out.

Changing the plan during a project

The initial plan is used to scope out upcoming iterations. A definitive set of stories is selected for an iteration just before it starts, and they are discussed in detail and precisely scoped out. We leave out features that will be developed and delivered later. When the current set have been implemented, the customers or product owners have a chance to revisit the plan, potentially modifying the priorities and shuffling things around for the next iteration.

On longer projects, the customer's business requirements or market circumstances often change during the implementation, so parts of the original specification become obsolete halfway through the project. Working out a detailed specification for a twelve-month project before development is a sure way to waste a lot of time discussing functionality that will become obsolete. Because there are no details in user stories, we can easily change the plan later without wasting too much time and effort. We won't have spent weeks working on the details of features that might become irrelevant in the future. A plan based on user stories facilitates change rather then impedes it.

In a sense, *stories are just reminders for discussion and placeholders in the project plan.* Before the development actually starts, we need to have a proper discussion about what a story entails and flesh out the details for development.

User stories and acceptance tests

User stories provide a high level plan and facilitate discussion, but they do not specify any details. Agile acceptance tests, on the other hand, provide specification details but do not even try to put things into a wider perspective. Used together, these two techniques complement each other.

A key idea of user stories is that we postpone a detailed discussion until we really need to start working on a particular story, to reduce the overhead of change. Postponing the discussion about details also allows us to utilise the knowledge we gained developing previous stories. This is a major distinction between user stories and more traditional planning methods. If the entire scope and requirements are captured only at the beginning of the project, you cannot use any of the knowledge or insights that you acquire only during development.

When the time comes to have the detailed discussion, we have a specification workshop (described in detail in Chapter 4). A workshop takes place at the start of every iteration, once the stakeholders have chosen a set of stories that they would like it to cover. Before the workshop, a story is just a placeholder for discussion. During the workshop, we take the story and discuss it at length. After the workshop, we have detailed requirements and specifications in the form of examples, built just in time for the development to start.

The specification workshop, in a sense, continues where the user stories leave off. User stories summarise ideas about the project and schedule them. The specification workshop is where we elaborate these ideas and specify exactly what they entail. User stories drive each workshop and examples defined during it become the acceptance criteria for an implementation of a story. The discussion that takes place during the workshop ensures that customers, domain experts and the implementation team share an understanding of what the story requires. The acceptance tests produced based on the examples coming out of the workshop allow developers to focus their work and testers to verify the story implementation.

Mary Poppendieck says that the worst waste of software development is adding features that are not needed to get the customers' job done[21]. User stories, with their focus on customer benefits and user roles that actually benefit from them, give us an excellent framework to focus the discussion during the workshop. A plan based on stories tells us exactly what we need to focus on for the next iteration and which benefits we need to fulfill. Having this clearly defined helps focus the specification workshop on particular customer expectations, giving us a platform to discuss which examples are really important for this phase of development and which should be left for later. This helps a lot to eliminate 'just-in-case' code.

In essence, user stories are the *scope* for the project, facilitating long-term planning and helping us get the big picture of what needs to be done. Acceptance tests are the detailed *specifications* that are ironed out only before the implementation of a particular story or a set of related stories. With regard to 'three Cs of user stories', the specification workshop is the conversation and acceptance tests coming out of the workshop are the confirmation.

Stuff to remember

- Agile acceptance testing and user stories complement each other incredibly well.
- You do not have to plan projects with user stories, but there are significant benefits if you intend to introduce agile acceptance testing.
- User stories focus on customer benefits, so it is easier for customers to plan based on them.
- Group stories into deliverables by business goals and make sure that each deliverable can go to production.
- User stories are the scope. Acceptance tests are the specification.

Chapter 10
Tools of today

Agile acceptance testing relies on test automation, so much so that the tools that we use for automation dictate the form in which tests are recorded and guide us in development. In this chapter, I describe several tools that you can use for test automation while still keeping tests in a form that can be understood by both business people and software implementation teams.

Tools and technologies come and go, but ideas and practices stay with us. In fact, the incompleteness of today's tools is one of the major obstacles to the adoption of agile acceptance testing. I expect tools to improve considerably in the near future, so giving you detailed instructions on how to use them in this book would not be effective. You will be able to find more complete and more up-to-date user manuals for tools online.

Instead, I want to present an overview of some of the most popular or interesting tools offered today, as a short tourist guide that will inspire you to explore further and tell you where to look for more information. This chapter is a bit technical, so feel free to skip parts of it if you are only interested in the business side of the story.

FIT

Framework for Integrated Testing (FIT) was the first popular acceptance testing framework, originally developed for Java by Ward Cunningham in 2002. At that time, Ward Cunningham called it "a tool for enhancing collaboration in software development".[1] One of the central ideas of FIT was to promote collaboration and allow customers, testers and programmers to write and verify acceptance tests together.

---

[1] http://fit.c2.com/

FIT works with a tabular model for describing tests. A typical FIT test is shown in Figure 10.1. Test inputs and expected results are specified in a table, with expected outcomes ending with a question mark in the column headings. This tabular form makes it very easy to write and review tests. Results are presented in the same format. If a particular expected value does not match the actual outcome, FIT marks the cell red and prints out both the expected and actual value. FIT simply ignores everything outside of the tables, so additional documentation, project notes, diagrams and explanations can be easily bundled with acceptance tests, providing deeper insight into the problem domain and helping people understand and verify test results. All this helps to evolve tests with the code more easily.

Figure 10.1. A typical FIT test table

The prize pool is divided among the winners using the following distribution for winning combinations (number of correct hits out of six chosen numbers). The example below is for $2M payout pool.

Prize Distribution for Payout Pool	2,000,000	
Winning Combination	Pool Percentage?	Prize Pool?
6	68	1,360,000
5	10	200,000
4	10	200,000
3	12	240,000

These tabular tests are excellent for calculation rules, but they are not really good for describing workflows or stories. Rick Mugridge has developed an extension to FIT called FitLibrary that allows us to specify flow tests as stories in a format similar to English prose (see Figure 10.2). Although it is technically a separate extension, FitLibrary is now considered by most people to be part of the standard set of test types. FIT and FitLibrary together provide about ten different ways to specify tests with tables, including lists, sets, stories and calculations based on column and row headings. This makes FIT very flexible and because of this it remains the most popular tool for acceptance testing despite much recent competition.

Figure 10.2. FitLibrary flow test

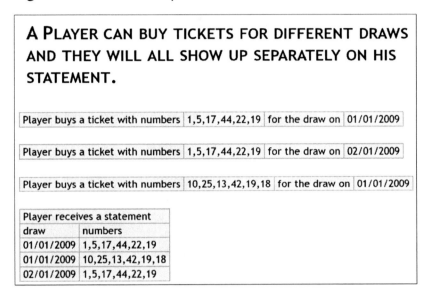

FIT tables connect to the domain code using a very thin glue code layer. These layers are called *fixtures*. A fixture is effectively more an integration API then a testing API. The fixture tells FIT how to interpret a particular table, where to assign input arguments, how to execute a test and where to read actual test outputs. The example in Figure 10.3 is a Column Fixture, which maps table columns to public fields, properties and methods of the fixture class. In general, FIT requires very little extra code for testing – just enough to provide a sanity check for the underlying interfaces. Often, FIT fixtures constitute the first client of our code.

Figure 10.3. FIT fixtures are the glue between tables and domain code

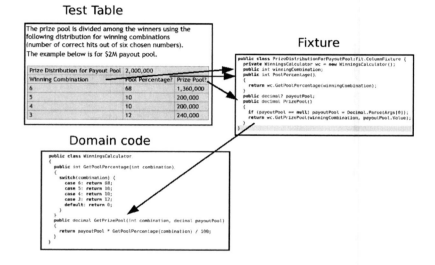

FitNesse

FIT makes it easy to run tests, but does not provide a way to create or manage them. The original idea was to write tests in Word, Excel, or any tool that can output HTML. FitNesse (see Figure 10.4) is a web wiki front-end to FIT developed by Robert C. Martin and Micah Martin of Object Mentor in 2005. Today it is the most popular choice for running FIT tests. It provides an integrated environment in which we can write and execute tests and speeds up the job with quite a few useful shortcuts. Although FitNesse is also written in Java, it is not heavily integrated with FIT, but executes it as an external program. This is very useful, as it enables us to plug in different test runners. After the FIT-FitNesse combination became popular in the Java world, test runners were written for other environments including C++, Python, .NET and SmallTalk. FitNesse is a web-based server, allowing easy collaboration. Business analysts and other non-technical people do not have to set up any software in order to use FitNesse. Any browser will do just fine. FitNesse also allows us to organise tests into test suites, reuse a shared set-up or tear-down for the entire test suite and include test components, making tests easier to manage and maintain long-term.

Figure 10.4. FitNesse is a web wiki front-end to FIT

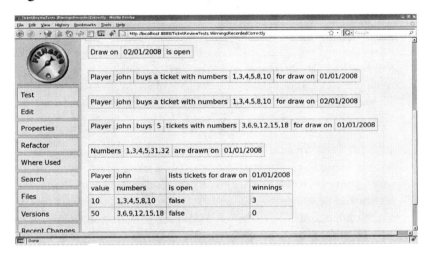

However, it is not without its problems. FitNesse was designed as a stand-alone network server with its own version control system, but most people simply did not want to use it this way and continued to store tests in the main project version control system. Although the internal version control system in FitNesse can be turned off, because of the way that tests are stored on disk some of its features don't really work with folder-based version control systems such as Subversion and CVS. The way that tests are organised in FitNesse at the moment also does not scale well when you need to deal with thousands of tests in deep hierarchies.

In general, FIT and FitNesse have a relatively short learning curve and allow people to get started with acceptance testing really quickly. The tabular form of specifying tests is very concise and I personally prefer it to free-form text or keyword-based systems, although it is arguably not the best to describe workflows.

Alternative tools

A number of alternative test runners and test management tools for FIT have emerged in the last several years. FitClipse by DoubTech[2] is an Eclipse plug-in that manages FitNesse tests. BandXI also offer an Eclipse plug-in[3] that enables developers to start and stop FitNesse from Eclipse and execute tests. Jeremy D. Miller has written StoryTeller,[4] which provides a way to run and manage tests in Visual Studio. Rick Mugridge is working on ZiBreve,[5] a Java IDE for story tests with WYSIWYG editing and support for refactoring tests. Jay Flowers has written a plug-in[6] for TestDriven.NET that runs FitNesse tests from Visual Studio.

FIT, FitNesse and most of the supporting tools are open source. For people requiring commercial support and integration with commercial tools, there is Green Pepper[7] by Pyxis Software. Green Pepper is built on similar concepts to FIT and FitNesse, but it integrates nicely with Confluence and JIRA from Atlassian, providing a more integrated way of managing tests and relating them to development tasks and issues. An interesting feature of Green Pepper is that it supports multiple versions of a single test, so that you can mark which version is actually implemented and which version is being implemented for the next release, allowing you to manage more easily the transition from acceptance tests to regression tests and back.

More information

For more information on FIT and FitNesse, see *FIT for developing software*[9] by Rick Mugridge and Ward Cunningham and my book *Test Driven .NET Development with FitNesse*[22]. The *Fixture Gallery*[8]

---

[2] http://www.doubtech.com/development/software/projects/?project=1
[3] http://www.bandxi.com/fitnesse/index.html
[4] http://storyteller.tigris.org/
[5] http://www.zibreve.com/
[6] http://jayflowers.com/WordPress/?p=157
[7] http://www.greenpeppersoftware.com/en/products/
[8] http://sourceforge.net/projects/fixturegallery

is a free PDF guide that explains all the most popular test (fixture) types, offering advice on when to use them, when not to use them and how to save time and effort when writing tests. For more resources, see the main FitNesse web site http://www.fitnesse.org and the community-maintained public wiki http://www.fitnesse.info.

Concordion

Concordion, developed by David Peterson and released under the Apache open source license, is an interesting alternative to FIT. Like FIT, Concordion uses HTML documents as executable specifications and requires some glue code (also called fixture code) to connect the executable elements of the specification to the domain code. Unlike FIT, Concordion does not require the specification to be in any particular format – you can write examples as normal sentences, without any restrictions.

Concordion is really simple. Its instrumentation only allows programmers to set global test variables, execute fixture methods and compare actual results with expected values. Programmers can use special HTML element attributes to mark words or phrases that are used as test inputs or compared to test results. Web browsers just ignore unknown element attributes, so Concordion test instrument-ation is effectively invisible to people that are not interested in test automation. For repetitive specifications and calculation rules, Concordion also supports attributes for tables similar to those of the FIT Column Fixture.

Currently, Concordion only supports Java fixtures, since it actually works as a JUnit extension. This provides direct integration with JUnit test runners, making it much easier to execute Concordion tests from popular development environments and integrate them into continuous build systems. It also shortens the learning curve required to start using Concordion. The fixture is simply a JUnit test class, with the same name as the HTML file containing the test.

Concordion's fixture model does not depend on inheritance so it is easier to learn than FIT and more flexible. On the other hand, Concordion lacks the extensibility of FIT and its powerful type adapters and cell handlers that enable it to bind domain objects and business services directly to the specification.

When a test is executed, Concordion runs through the files and executes commands, comparing expected outputs with actual results. The JUnit test run tells you whether all tests passed or there were failures. Concordion also saves the results to disk in HTML, making it easier to see what actually went wrong. You can see an example of a test result on Figure 10.5.

Concordion does not have a test management tool and relies completely on the programmer's IDE to manipulate and execute tests. I have mixed feelings about this. Although file management within an IDE makes it much easier to put tests in the same version control system as the domain code, I miss the ability to use common set-ups and test components with macro variables such as are available in FitNesse. It also puts tests completely under the control of programmers.

Concordion takes some ideas that have evolved as best practices in the FIT-FitNesse arena and makes them very explicit, actively discouraging other ways of working. For example, acceptance tests have to be stored in the same folder structure as the code, making it easy to include them in the same version control system. There are no prebuilt test building blocks that would encourage people to re-use them, often leading to large unreadable test scripts (see the section *Distilling the specifications* on page 78).

What worries me slightly is that developers need to add non-standard HTML attributes to the test page. This smells to me of a hand-over of tests from business people to developers at some point, which is a practice that I don't approve of at all. In my opinion, tests should be shared between the whole team and not handed over. I am sure that the problem can be avoided with some discipline, and there are probably visual HTML editors which business people can use that will not ruin hidden test instrumentation, but I would still like to see a proper test management tool for business people and testers. Exposing tests in an IDE is great for developers, as they can debug and troubleshoot tests easily, but testers and business people need to view tests at a higher level.

Figure 10.5. Concordion works with any text in a HTML document

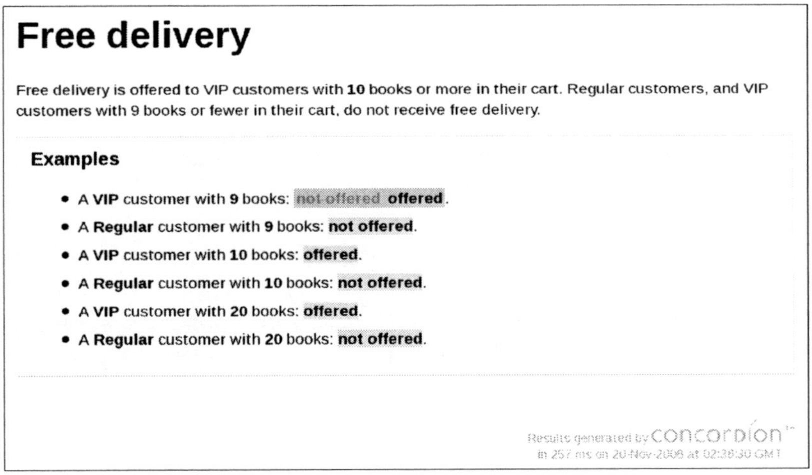

Free delivery

Free delivery is offered to VIP customers with **10** books or more in their cart. Regular customers, and VIP customers with 9 books or fewer in their cart, do not receive free delivery.

Examples

- A **VIP** customer with **9** books: ~~not offered~~ **offered**.
- A **Regular** customer with **9** books: **not offered**.
- A **VIP** customer with **10** books: **offered**.
- A **Regular** customer with **10** books: **not offered**.
- A **VIP** customer with **20** books: **offered**.
- A **Regular** customer with **20** books: **not offered**.

Concordion has a really good web site with a helpful tutorial and lots of examples. For more information on this tool, and to download links and examples, see http://concordion.org.

JBehave

JBehave is the original behaviour-driven development tool, written for Java by Dan North, Liz Keogh, Mauro Talevi and Shane Duan. Behaviour-driven development uses a specific format of test scripts specified in the given-when-then format (see the section *Working with business workflows* on page 57). Here is a typical JBehave test script, taken from the JBehave source code repository:

```
Given a stock of prices 0.5,1.0
When the stock is traded at 2.0
Then the alert status should be OFF
When the stock is traded at 5.0
Then the alert status should be OFF
When the stock is traded at 11.0
Then the alert status should be ON
```

In a similar way to Concordion, JBehave plugs itself into the JUnit unit testing tool and works on a text file with the same name as the fixture class. In the JBehave jargon, both the series of given-when-then steps and the related glue code between test scripts and domain code are called a *scenario*. Individual elements of the given-when-then workflow are called *steps*. Each step is implemented as a Java method and annotations are used to match lines of text from the test script to the methods and their arguments.

JBehave test scripts are in plain English, making them really easy to understand. There is no hidden test instrumentation, which means that test scripts are easy to maintain and that business people can use any text editor or word processor to maintain the scripts. This also means that there is no way to specify lots of related specifications in a compact format such as a FIT table. I find that the given-when-then format is better for describing workflows and unique cases, whereas FIT tables are better for describing calculations and state-machine changes with lots of related rules.

Much of what I've written about Concordion applies to JBehave as well. Since JUnit is used under the hood, JBehave has a shorter learning curve technically and it integrates instantly with almost every IDE, build tool and continuous integration system. Test scripts are kept in the same folder structure and source code control system as the production code. There is no specific test management tool and test scripts are primarily under the control of the programmer's IDE.

JBehave feels much more like JUnit than any other tool described here, so if you are a programmer and want to start diving into acceptance testing, it might be the easiest one to learn. Compared to JUnit, it has test scripts externalised into text files and changes the language from *tests* and *assertions* to what the domain code *should* do, emphasising the fact that a test in this case is a specification. Unlike Concordion, the test script instrumentation is in the fixture class. This means that test scripts are unaffected by code refactoring, but it also means that you have to write a lot more code than with Concordion. Unlike Concordion, there is no standard way to specify lots of related examples with table attributes. You can, however, extend the way JBehave parses scenarios by implementing your own converter to handle such cases. Currently JBehave developers are working on a standard extension that would allow you to specify related examples as a table under the 'other examples include' heading.[9]

You can download JBehave from http://jbehave.org. If you are not using Java, there are similar tools for different platforms and programming languages. In fact, the Ruby version, RSpec, seems to be a lot more popular among Ruby programmers than JBehave is in the Java community. At the Agile 2008 conference a new Ruby BDD tool called Cucumber was announced, with two very interesting features. The first is support for internationalisation, making it easier to apply BDD in another language besides English. The second interesting innovation is the ability to supply additional combinations of inputs and expected outputs for a scenario using a simple table syntax appended to the classic RSpec scenario template, very similar to a classic FIT column fixture. This could make writing and maintaining BDD tests much easier as you would no longer have to copy and paste scenario descriptions to use different arguments.

TextTest

TextTest is a tool for 'managing system behaviour changes' written by Geoff Bache, and it stands out from all the other tools mentioned here because of its way of working and its unique feature set. Geoff Bache explains[10] it as a move away from trying to write a sequence of assertions that entirely describes the correct behaviour of the program:

---

[9]http://www.testingreflections.com/node/view/7339
[10]in a private e-mail

Systems change over time and so does their behaviour: why not have a testing tool that assumes this as normal? This view seems to me entirely in line with an agile view of software development, though it is a bit of paradigm shift if you're used to testing with assertions and APIs [...] I don't see this as different or mutually exclusive to testing in development (if a program isn't in development, there isn't so much point testing it). My attitude is that however incomplete the program, it does something today that is better than nothing: so we manage the changes in its behaviour and make sure that we always move forwards, never backwards, when we change the code.

Unlike FIT and Concordion, which inspect the system using an integration fixture API, TextTest inspects the system by analysing log files and other outputs generated during test runs and and comparing them to expected results. Because of this, TextTest is much better for verifying business workflows and integrations. FIT and Concordion can only confirm the results of a function call through the external API. TextTest can confirm that the correct process was executed during the function call, by analysing individual steps and verifying the flow of information.

TextTest also supports multiple active versions of the same test and integrates with xUseCase tools for recording and replaying user interface tests. xUseCase libraries differ from standard UI recorders because they associate recorded actions with use case command names rather than captured UI system events. Use case commands are named in domain terms, as suggested by business people, testers and developers. Test scripts can then be written using these domain-specific names, not by capturing system events. This allows us to focus user interface test scripts on what the system is intended to do in terms of the domain, without getting involved in implementation details. The result is that xUseCase scripts are much easier to understand and manipulate and are much closer to the domain. This is similar to the domain-specific testing language approach of Mickey Phoenix and SolutionsIQ, explained in the section *Don't describe business rules through the user interface* on page 91. TextTest integrates with PyUseCase[11] and JUseCase[12] providing this user-interface recording functionality to Python and Java programs.

Although TextTest is intended to be primarily a regression test tool, it allows us to define future business workflows as sentences in a text file and then use them as acceptance tests for development. In the context of the topic of this book, the most interesting features of TextTest are its ability to analyse business workflows and its domain-oriented user interface recording and replay functions.

Since it works on text files, TextTest can inspect software written in any language on any platform, so if you are working in a legacy environment or with a non-standard platform, TextTest might be your only choice for acceptance testing. It could also prove useful as a tool for retrofitting regression tests into a legacy system, because it is much less intrusive than tools that depend on an external API.

In addition to functional testing, TextTest has some unique features such as built-in performance test support and the ability to record and replay messages to other programs or systems to help mock out external dependencies for testing.

TextTest has a console interface for automation and a graphical interface for easier use (see Figure 10.6). The graphical interface also serves as a test management tool, allowing you to group tests into hierarchies. TextTest is itself written in Python, so it can be extended by writing Python modules that preprocess or postprocess inputs and outputs to customise the test execution for your particular application.

To get the most out of this approach to testing, the key is to create logs with an appropriate level of detail. Geoff Bache recommends that good logs should be:

- as readable as possible for someone who knows the system but not the code

---

[11]http://sourceforge.net/projects/pyusecase/
[12]http://jusecase.sourceforge.net/

- detailed enough to describe the important things that the system does

- not so detailed that they become hard to read and excessively volatile

This ultimately leads to much more focus on designing the log files and having logs that are understandable to non-programmers. I find this side-effect very interesting, as it should make log files much more usable for support and troubleshooting in production as well.

For more information on TextTest, see http://www.texttest.org/. I especially recommend the *Publications* page, which has slides from Geoff Bache's presentation from the Agile 2008 conference and the Minesweeper Kata screencast.

Figure 10.6. TextTest graphical user interface

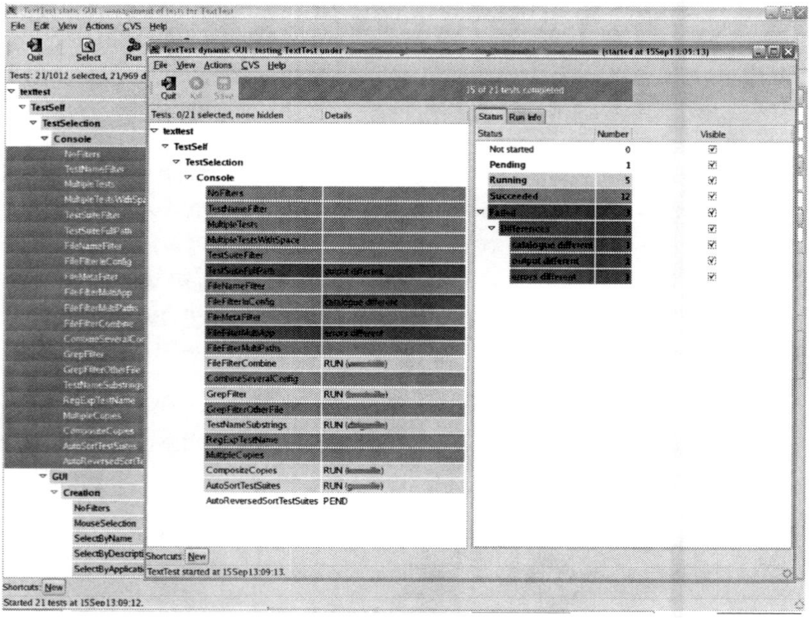

Selenium

Selenium is a web browser automation tool that can manipulate and validate HTML document object model elements. The three most common uses of Selenium are automating web user interface tests, verifying web site compatibility with various browsers and platforms and periodically checking whether a site is online and works correctly. In the context of the topic of this book, Selenium is interesting as an engine that drives acceptance tests through the user interface.

The Selenium project started as a JavaScript functional test runner in 2004 created by Jason Huggins, Paul Gross and Jie Tina Wang, who were working for ThoughtWorks at the time. It is an open source product, actively maintained by ThoughtWorks, with a large community of supporters. Since 2004, it has significantly evolved in terms of functionality and tool support. In fact, additional tool support and integration options are two of the best features of Selenium.

The core of Selenium is written in JavaScript and HTML and it is compatible with all major browsers, including Internet Explorer and Firefox. It runs on Windows, Linux and Mac. Selenium works by embedding control scripts into a browser window frame and automating another window frame with the scripts. An example Selenium screen is shown in Figure 10.7. The top half of the screen is the Selenium control interface: the top-left corner shows the current test suite, the middle part shows the current test and the top-right corner contains the panel that controls tests. The bottom part of the screen shows the web site under test.

Selenium test scripts are written as tables, with table rows representing test steps. The first cell in a row contains a command keyword, the second and third cells contain command arguments. This test language is known as Selenese. For an example that submits a search form and validates the output, see Figure 10.8. Selenese has many different keywords to simulate clicks, type text into fields, load pages, evaluate text in elements, check for alerts and manipulate and inspect HTML element properties.[13] Selenium can identify document object model (DOM) elements based on their IDs, names and XPath expressions, so its test language is very flexible in terms of working with HTML pages. You don't have to be a programmer to write Selenium scripts, but you do need technical knowledge about the DOM and Selenese is very low-level and technical. Therein lies one of the biggest problems with Selenium. Writing and maintaining Selenium scripts by hand is probably not the best idea, even if you are a programmer, because small changes in the user interface can break many tests. Because of this, Selenium is rarely used on its own. It is mostly combined with other test management tools or wrapped into interfaces that make test scripts easier to use and maintain.

Figure 10.7. Selenium test runner

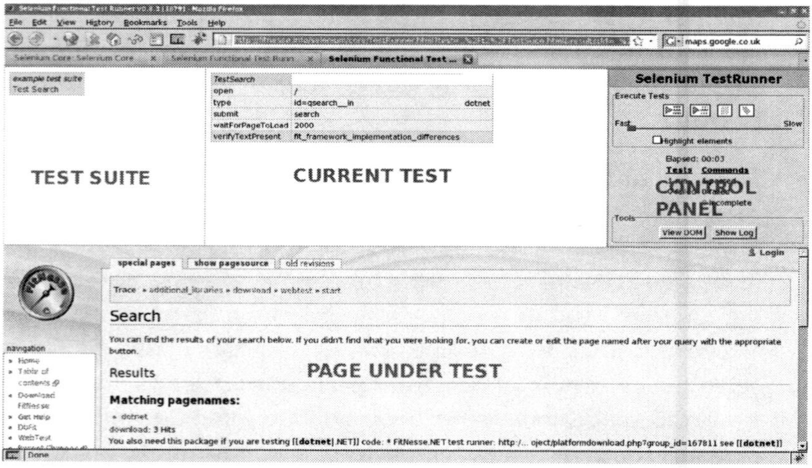

Selenium has a visual test automation tool that supports record-and-replay operations, called *Selenium IDE* (see Figure 10.9). The tool is aimed at less technical people who do not want to write Selenese scripts by hand and works as a Firefox plug-in (Internet explorer is not supported currently). The Selenium IDE comes with good

---

[13] see http://selenium-core.openqa.org/reference.html for more information

command reference documentation, point-and-click helpers and the ability to save and load tests from the disk.

Figure 10.8. A typical Selenium test

TestSearch		
open	/	
type	id=qsearch_in	dotnet
submit	search	
waitForPageToLoad	2000	
verifyTextPresent	fit_framework_implementation_differences	

For more flexible automation, there is *Selenium Remote Control*. Remote Control is an add-on that provides the glue between the core browser automation engine and .NET, Java or Python code. It works as a Java server process that accepts commands over TCP and launches a browser to execute them. Remote Control enables us to write and run Selenium tests from almost all popular test frameworks, combining them with integration test functions that prepare, clean up or validate domain objects. It also allows us to remotely execute Selenium tests on dedicated machines, making it possible to automatically run the same test in multiple browsers on different operating systems.

The biggest problem of Selenium Remote Control is speed of execution – the interface between the Remote Control server and JavaScript running in a browser is a real performance hog and makes it very ineffective to run Selenium-based tests as part of the basic build process. A possible solution for this problem in the Java world is to use TestNG with parallel test execution. The Selenium Grid project is another possible solution. It automatically distributes Selenium tests across multiple machines and comes with built-in support for Amazon's EC2 Cloud.

Download Selenium from http://www.openqa.org. There you will also find find code examples, a command reference and installation and usage instructions for the core library, Remote Control and Selenium Grid.

Figure 10.9. The Selenium IDE allows testers to record and replay tests

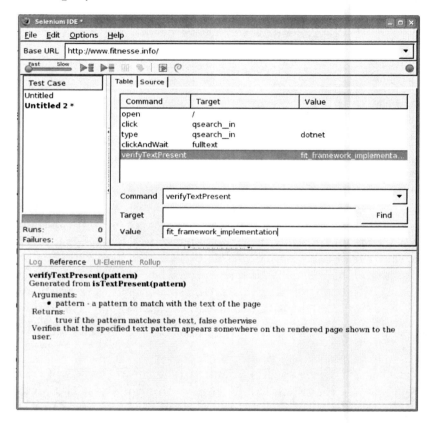

Tools based on Selenium

CubicTest is an interesting tool that allows us to write and manage Selenium tests as visual page transitions (see Figure 10.10). It also offers the ability to generate mock web sites based on test scripts, so it might be an interesting tool for prototyping user interface workflows. CubicTest is an open source plug-in for the popular Eclipse IDE. For more information and to download, see http://www.cubictest.com.

StoryTestIQ, a wiki-based Selenium test management system by SolutionsIQ, is a mixture of Selenium and FitNesse. It offers easier test management and the ability to run SQL commands to prepare the database for testing through the user interface. It integrates with continuous integration tools. You can download StoryTestIQ from http://storytestiq.solutionsiq.com.

Figure 10.10. CubicTest manages tests as visual page transitions

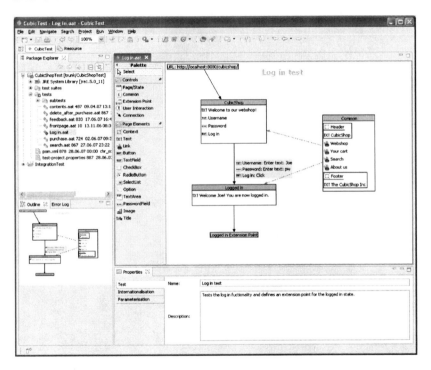

WebTest fixtures are a library of additional FIT fixtures for Java and .NET which I wrote to allow business analysts and testers to specify Selenium tests without actually learning the Selenese language. The fixtures convert English sentences such as 'user clicks on Cancel' and 'Page contains text Hello Mike' into Selenium Remote Control commands, enabling non-programmers to write and maintain user interface tests from FitNesse. For more information, see http://fitnesse.info/webtest.

 Stuff to remember

- There are many different acceptance testing tools today on the market.
- Start by evaluating FIT–FitNesse, Concordion and JBehave for business domain testing.
- Selenium, CubicTest and StoryTestIQ might help you with UI tests.
- To maintain UI tests more easily, use page objects or domain-specific keywords to describe actions in a business language.
- TextTest can be an interesting choice for inspecting workflows and building up regression test suites for existing systems.

Chapter 11
Tools of tomorrow

Tool support for agile acceptance testing is today good enough for us to get our work done, but not good enough for our work to be really efficient. Early adopters of the practice were forgiving and ready to overlook problems with tools, working around them or implementing their own solutions. However for this practice to become widespread, we need better tools that give us a shorter learning curve and allow us to do our jobs more efficiently. As the practice evolves, the tools need to evolve too. Here are some ideas that I would really like to see in our tools in the near future.

Domain-specific languages

The idea of *domain-specific languages* (DSL) seems to be gaining a lot of momentum currently. The basic idea is to create a specific mini-programming language, often based on some action-oriented keywords, focused on a particular business domain and even tailored to the needs of a particular customer. We then use this mini-language to describe business processes and constraints. Business people and domain experts can then effectively participate in programming – even if they don't want to write in the language themselves, they will at least be able to read and understand it. So domain-specific languages can improve communication in a project. Another rationale behind this idea is that domain-specific language constructs allow us to describe the business problem more efficiently than with general-purpose languages. The mini-language is ultimately implemented in a general purpose language such as Java or C#, so that process definitions written in the business language can be integrated with the infrastructure.

This idea is very close to the concept of writing acceptance tests so that business people can understand them. In agile acceptance testing, the acceptance tests are written in business language and serve as a specification for the code. Verifications and actions related to the business language keywords are then implemented in a general-purpose language, for example Java or C#.

A domain-specific language does not have to be based on keywords in text. FIT, Concordion and similar tools actually already give us a way to use domain-specific languages without calling them by this name. FIT, for example, enables us to use tables to create a DSL. The automation part (the fixtures) can be viewed as an implementation of the domain-specific language described by the constructs used in acceptance tests.

With some lower-level tools such as user interface recorders, tests are described as series of small technical steps, making it hard to see the wood for the trees. Some companies such as SolutionsIQ are pioneering the idea of domain-specific testing languages – applying the idea of domain-specific languages to encapsulate technical complexity into something that business people can read and write. The constructs of such languages are used to describe user-interface acceptance tests in a form readable by business people. The implementation of the constructs encapsulates all the technical details, hiding them in the code. Instead of a web page test script with thirty steps to populate and submit a registration form, confirm terms and conditions and verify that the registered e-mail address is correct, we might just use the 'register-customer' keyword in the test specification. The benefits of this approach are better readability and easier management and maintenance of acceptance tests. Developers can use domain-specific keywords to discuss tests with business people and user interface changes will be localised to individual keyword implementations, they will not propagate to domain tests. As user-interface testing tools evolve and speed up, this idea might prove to be more and more interesting. Some automation tools such as JUseCase and PyUseCase provide the infrastructure for this for thick-client applications.

As agile acceptance testing gains in popularity this concept will surely evolve. Domain-specific languages and their counterparts in testing are aleady becoming more and more popular – witness the support for dynamic languages in Microsoft's .NET CLR and the increasing number of Java JRE-based languages.

Adam Geras held a talk during the second Agile Alliance Functional Testing Tools workshop, during which he suggested that instead of a testing tool or framework a good future base for acceptance testing using domain-specific languages would be a new virtual machine.[1] The virtual machine would provide support for different testing contexts, including test-first, test-after and exploratory testing. Such a virtual machine would give us full flexibility to write tests and specifications in domain-specific languages, but would not impose any specific functional form or limitations.

Different user interfaces for different roles

Current test management tools try to provide a compromise between technical efficiency and user-friendliness in order to be usable by developers, testers and business people. Jennitta Andrea has written an article called *Envisioning the Next Generation of Functional Testing Tools*[2] in which she suggests that future tools should provide better, more focused interfaces for different people depending on their roles. Jennitta writes that a functional test has to be easier to read and locate than code. In addition, as a single test often describes just a part of a business rule, related tests have to be easy to locate and review.

Different people expect different things from a test. Business people and domain experts are mostly concerned with verifying the correctness of the specification in the test. Testers are mostly concerned with running the test and getting meaningful execution results. They also want an efficient way to identify and describe bugs. Developers are concerned with understanding the test as a specification for development or bug-fixing. Business analysts and developers are often

---

[1] http://video.google.com/videoplay?docid=-6298610650460170080&hl=en
[2] See [23]. Also see http://www.jennittaandrea.com/wp-content/uploads/2007/04/envisioningthenextgenerationoffunctionaltestingtools_ieeesw_may2007.pdf.

concerned just with the current state of tests, not so much about the previous test runs. Testers are typically interested in the results of earlier test executions and previous versions of tests as well.

I'm not so sure that all these roles can be reconciled in a single user interface, and I'd like to see multiple user interfaces that focus on providing the best individual benefits for particular roles. For example, I would expect better integration with traditional integrated development environments for programmers, so that they can debug and troubleshoot code under test while they are implementing parts of a specification or bug-fixing. Testers, on the other hand, should not have to run tests from a programmer IDE, but from an interface that gives them a quicker global overview with fewer details. Business people should be able to write and review tests in a visual WYSIWYG environment similar to a word processor or spreadsheet. I would like future tools not to attempt to be all things to all men, but to provide all the features that a particular user needs to do his job efficiently, while allowing others to use different tools.

Even though some IDEs such as Eclipse offer a rich client application development framework, I still think that applications based on IDE frameworks are too technical for business people to use, and that we need a proper business view of the tests. After all, this is why FitNesse is still the most popular test management system for FIT tests in spite of all its problems.

Propagating the effects of changes

Refactoring is the practice of improving the design of existing code without changing its functionality, today regarded as one of the key agile development practices. If you are not a technical person, consider it as periodic house-cleaning after development. The comparison is not entirely correct because refactoring is typically a continuous process and not a once-off effort, but it is good enough for our purposes. Most integrated development environments today support refactoring automation, so that changes are automatically propagated to related files. For example, when part of an object is extracted into a new object, or when a function name is changed, the change is automatically implemented in all the places where the object or the function are used. This automation makes such changes much cheaper and less error prone.

Unfortunately, since acceptance test descriptions are not kept in the code but in external files, such refactoring does not affect acceptance tests. Some tools decouple the test description from the code using test fixtures. Automated tools propagate changes applied in the domain code to the fixture code as well, while leaving the fixture interface unchanged. This allows tests to still pass after refactoring, but the language in the tests is no longer consistent with the language in the domain. This makes tests harder to understand and goes against the principle of using a consistent ubiquitous language on the project.

With tools that skip the fixture part and hook test scripts directly to domain objects or analyse the raw unprocessed output of domain classes, refactoring domain code breaks the tests.

In both cases, tests need to be updated to be kept consistent with the domain code. Regardless of the tool, acceptance tests become out-of-date after code refactoring. Currently they need to be fixed manually. This is one of the major pain areas of acceptance testing today.

ThoughtWorks were working on a tool called Profit[3] that converted FitNesse tests to Java code, which would be affected by refactoring, but this project seems to have been abandoned. The last update was more than two years ago and it was still marked as 'in planning'. However, this is an interesting idea, although I suspect that turning tests into code will make them much more technical and less understandable. While I was writing this book, ThoughtWorks have announced plans to release a new tool called Twist[4] that promises to bring better refactoring support.

I expect that future tools will have much better support for refactoring, plugging into the integrated development environments and automat-

---

[3]http://sourceforge.net/projects/profit
[4]http://studios.thoughtworks.com/twist-agile-test-automation/

ically propagating changes to acceptance tests. This could work both ways, with business people updating tests and these updates propagating to the domain code.

Direct domain mapping

Most acceptance testing tools today allow us to describe tests in a human-understandable language and then have a translation layer that converts it into domain API calls. Acceptance tests are a really good way to create and evolve an ubiquitous language for the project, which helps a great deal to improve communication between business people and technical people on the team (see the section *Building a domain language* on page 66 and the section *Evolve the language consistently* on page 134). Using this approach, both the domain code and acceptance tests use the same names and constructions, so the translation API becomes just boiler-plate code, but it is still code that has to be written and maintained.

Both FIT.NET and Java FitLibrary have started to move towards using a rich domain model that is more effective than the traditional mapping of each step into a fixture or a DoFixture method. Domain fixtures and domain adapters in FIT.NET and Java FitLibrary utilise rich domain objects without the need to write boiler-plate fixtures. These mappings are still in the early stages of development and are not comprehensive – adapters still have to be written for specific domains. During the Agile 2008 conference, Mike Stockdale organised a mini-session where he and Rick Mugridge presented some new features and ideas that they were working on at the time. The session led to a very interesting discussion on whether we could produce types of domain adapters and domain fixtures that would allow FIT to connect directly to most domain services and objects without the need for any fixtures.

Moving forward in this direction, this approach would allow acceptance test automation tools to directly utilise domain-driven design concepts such as repositories, business services, entities and value objects. This would remove the need to implement any generic fixtures to connect test scripts to domain code. Only genuine test-specific code would need to be developed and maintained. By eliminating the translation layer, this approach also promotes the use of the ubiquitous language.

A major problem with connecting test scripts directly to domain code at the moment is that it makes tests harder to maintain, because test scripts are not isolated from changes in the code. On the other hand, test scripts and domain code have to be kept synchronised anyway to make the most of the ubiquitous project language approach, even if they are isolated. Better support for IDE integration and refactoring will make test scripts easier to maintain, allowing us to obtain in full the benefits of directly connecting to the domain. For some ideas that came out of the workshop during Agile 2008, see my article *FIT without Fixtures*.[5]

Better editors

During the second Agile Alliance Functional Testing Tools workshop, Elisabeth Hendrickson called for better editor tools rather then just support for refactoring.[6] Her idea was that future tools must reduce the cost of changing tests, allowing us to efficiently reconcile new expectations with those already expressed as acceptance tests. Better editors will reduce the cost of change and facilitate change in tests rather then impede it. Elisabeth Hendrickson pointed out two key features that future editors should have:

- They should allow people to quickly identify mismatches between expectations in their minds and those written down as acceptance tests.

- They should make it easy to change tests to reconcile mismatches easily and quickly.

With better editors like these, the lack of support for carrying through refactoring into acceptance tests would not be such a problem, because

---

[5]http://gojko.net/2008/08/12/fit-without-fixtures/
[6]http://video.google.com/videoplay?docid=8565239121902737883&hl=en

we could easily implement changes in acceptance tests to reflect domain changes after refactoring.

Jennitta Andrea has suggested[23] that better test editors should provide intelligent language support that works with domain-specific testing languages, in the same way as intelligent code helpers work in developer tools.

Better test organisation

FitNesse has an internal version control system that has turned out to be more of a stumbling-block than a useful feature. Most people want to keep tests and domain source code in the same repository under the management of a single version control system. Other tools don't even try to tackle this issue and rely on the IDE to handle version management. A key feature of future tools, especially if they offer multiple views of the same tests, has to be proper version control integration with popular source-code control systems. A FitNesse plug-in intended to allow this has been in development for a few years, but as of now it is still not complete. This feature is not so important for programmers, because most IDEs already support many version control systems. But it will be a key feature of business-oriented and tester-oriented interfaces to acceptance testss.

In addition to this, future tools need to support multiple active versions of a single test. A single version of the test for each branch of source code is not enough. With acceptance tests that facilitate a change to a system, we might use several versions of the same test with the same source code branch. One version would describe what is currently implemented and be used for regression testing. A second version would describe where we want to be once the change is implemented and be used for guiding development. At the moment, having two versions of a single test often requires copying the test into a development space and then having two copies of the same file, with testers and the continuous integration environment focusing on the old file and developers working with the new file. Green Pepper and TextTest have direct support for multiple test versions, so that we can mark a revision as implemented or in development and then just execute tests marked with a particular version. I would like to see this feature in other test management tools as well, because it would make test management much easier.

Rick Mugridge has started work to implement test tags for SuiteFixture in FitLibrary. Test tags are arbitrary categories that can be assigned to tests so that we can list, execute and group tests, providing a more flexible mechanism to manage tests then the traditional file-system-based hierarchy. I would really like to see this implemented in test management tools such as FitNesse rather then in a library-specific test runner like FitLibrary. Test tags woule meet Jennitta Andrea's requirement that related tests should be easy to locate.

Visual workflow descriptions

Workflows are, at the moment, hard to describe and check properly with current acceptance testing tools. Most people are used to discussing and designing workflows with visual diagrams, but today's tools require us to describe workflows as sequences of steps in text. This makes it much harder to understand even simple straightforward workflows. Flows with lots of branches and conditionals, described as text steps, truly exemplify the proverb that a picture is worth a thousand words. Pictures are definitely a more effective way to design and communicate workflows. However, currently they are not executable.

One of the areas where acceptance testing tools will probably evolve in the future is visual workflow exploration and specification. Some tools for this already exist. CubicTest, described in the section *Tools based on Selenium* on page 190, has a visual page transition model to specify web workflows. Brian Marick has written a library that reads OmniGraffle graph documents and converts them into executable Ruby on Rails tests.[7]

---

[7]http://www.exampler.com/blog/2007/07/13/graphical-workflow-tests-for-rails/

Part IV. Effects on all of us

In this part, I try to answer the most common questions I get from business analysts, testers and developers on how agile acceptance testing will affect their roles. I also dispel common misconceptions and address fears and issues that people often have about agile acceptance testing because they have been misled by partial information.

Chapter 12
Effects on business analysts

During the QCon 2007 conference in London, Martin Fowler and Dan North organised a session called *The Crevasse of Doom*,[1] to discuss the communication gap between business users and software developers. Martin Fowler called this gap the biggest difficulty we face in software development today. He divided the strategies for crossing the gap into two groups: the ferry and the bridge.

The ferry is the traditional way to think about a communication problem. Fowler said that developers are often perceived to have poor communication skills, dress in T-shirts and talk in techno-jargon, so business people who dress in smart suits and talk in their business jargon think that they could not possibly communicate with developers. Professional intermediaries are hired as translators, who ferry information between the two groups. The problem with this approach is, as Fowler put it, that it is not a high-bandwidth form of communication and it makes no difference to the tradional gulf between developers and business people.

The bridge approach provides a structure that allows people to cross the gap directly, facilitating direct communication between the two groups. Instead of having professional translators, we work on fostering communication and building links between the two worlds, making a single world out of them. The bridge approach provides a much higher bandwidth and less distortion. It also offers an opportunity for people with different skills to work together to find better ways of solving business problems.

---

[1]http://www.infoq.com/presentations/Fowler-North-Crevasse-of-Doom

In the traditional requirements gathering process, a business analyst is a conduit of information. He or she is an expert hired by management to transfer and translate information because it is believed that developers and business people cannot understand each other. I think that this assumption is essentially flawed and I hope that, if you have read the preceding chapters, I have also convinced you to believe the same. This by no means makes the business analyst obsolete, but it affects the role that an analyst plays in the process. As Fowler put it, the traditional role of a business analyst is to be the ferry man. With agile acceptance testing, analysts become bridge builders. They are no longer the conveyor of information, but facilitators that enable people to share knowledge.

Rather than producing and handing over documents, the role of a business analyst is to organise the transfer of knowledge and chase open issues. The business analyst is a great choice for the facilitator of specification workshops. Very often, a business analyst is charged with owning and maintaining acceptance tests after workshops as well.

Benefits for business analysts

In the introduction, I listed six significant benefits of agile acceptance testing for business analysts. As a quick recap of Part II, let's look at these benefits again and see how the practices described deliver them.

Developers will actually read specifications

Ellen Gottesdiener wrote that collaborative requirements workshops commit participants to the workshop results more and promote their sense of ownership of the deliverables and the system ([19] Ch. 1). Because developers participate in specification workshops, they take a much more active part in the whole process. Instead of just passively reading the documents, they participate in writing the specifications so they understand them and are much more committed to them.

Because acceptance tests provide a focus for development and they are typically implemented one set at a time, you can be sure that each and every part of the specification will be thoroughly read and implemented completely.

They will understand the specifications correctly

Specification workshops facilitate discussion and allow the developers to give feedback on the specifications and examples. Realistic examples leave very little space for misunderstanding. By communicating intent and discussing goals and anti-goals you make sure that everyone sees the big picture. Feedback from developers and their participation in working through examples will give you confidence that they understood you correctly, or reveal areas of conflict that need to be explored further. No workshop ends until both you and the developers agree that you understand the same thing. The concrete examples contained in the set of acceptance tests help make sure that the system will do exactly what it is supposed to do, significantly reducing opportunities for ambiguity and misunderstandings.

They will not skip parts of the specifications

Specifications formulated as executable acceptance tests are impossible to skip over. If any part of the specification is not implemented, a test will fail and you'll know it straight away. Even better, developers will realise this themselves, so you don't need to get involved at all. Development does not end until all tests are green.

Because tests are based on precise examples, developers have to implement what is actually specified.

You can track development progress easily

The number of passing acceptance tests is a good realistic measure of how the project is progressing. It is not a perfect measure since it does not reflect infrastructure tasks, but as an approximation it is in practice very reliable. If a phase of development has 70 acceptance tests and only 20 of them are green, we are still in the first half of the phase. If you have 65 green tests, you know that you are almost done. Not all tests are of the same size and complexity, but in general the differences average out. With an automated test suite, you can easily run tests at any time and view progress. If a continuous integration server runs the tests for you overnight, you can get a useful e-mail report every morning.

You can easily identify conflicts in business rules

With a readily available set of tests focused on business rules, you can easily pull out tests related to a particular rule and compare them to a change request. You do not have to keep all the details of the initial specification and later changes in your head. Because the tests are connected directly to the code, if they execute correctly you can be sure that the specification in the acceptance tests is a reliable and authoritative statement of what has been implemented. Even if you do not compare the change request to all the relevant tests, any conflicting change of the code will break an existing regression test. Developers will notice a failed test straight away and alert you about it. This is why you will find about potential conflicts in change requests and specifications during development, not in production.

You'll save time on acceptance and smoke testing

When a reliable set of tests are executed periodically throughout the project and when each phase of the project is completed with a full, successful test run, you can be much more confident that the business rules are implemented in the code. You can easily execute the tests whenever you want. Because of this, you do not have to verify business rules manually before a delivery. You can still sanity-test the system to make sure that some obvious item did not get missed, but you do not have to spend a lot of time doing it. Knowing that the entire specification is correctly implemented will give you a lot of confidence in the code.

Challenges for business analysts

Here are some of the questions and concerns about agile acceptance testing I hear from business analysts during my talks, workshops and tutorials.

I don't do tests, that's not my job

Hopefully by now you have realised that acceptance tests are primarily a live specification of the system. Specifying what the software should do is definitely one of the responsibilities of a business analyst. If you let developers or testers work out acceptance tests on their own, you are not ensuring that the effective specification is correct so you will not be doing your job. If the word 'test' is a stumbling-block to understanding, use one of the alternatives suggested in the section *Better names* on page 38.

I find that realistic examples and specification workshops provide a much better framework for eliciting requirements with customers. They have to think at a more detailed level to provide concrete answers to concrete examples and they cannot just brush questions off. This helps significantly to discover the real business rules and to root out incorrect assumptions, so the customers will be less likely to change their minds later.

Not only is 'doing tests' part of a business analyst's job, but it makes the rest of your job much more effective.

It's extra work and I don't have time for that

Some people tend to keep working the way they feel comfortable with and pile up more work when they start doing agile acceptance testing. A business analyst who is comfortable with writing big specifications documents and lists of requirements might first write them and then organise a workshop to discuss examples. If such a process helps you organise your thoughts better or focus on details, I don't see a problem with it, although you will probably soon find out that the first part of the process can effectively be skipped. If there is an artefact to be considered as the physical output of a business analyst's work, then this should be a set of acceptance tests, not the requirements documents or abstract specifications. Maintaining both acceptance tests and requirements and synchronising them will take a lot of time and effort. Out of these, it is really important only to have acceptance tests up-to-date. So save time and just do acceptance tests.

With the specification workshop as an intensive hands-on laboratory in which we flush out all the inconsistencies and functionality gaps and build a shared understanding of the domain, you will actually spend much less time on transferring knowledge and communication.

If one of your responsibilities is to give the system a quick smoke test before a release, having a set of automated tests that check business rules will free up time for this.

But they will only look at the tests and not read the requirements...

Business analysts new to agile acceptance testing often complain about the fact that when acceptance tests are used as a target for development, developers disregard all other documents and focus only on the acceptance tests. This complaint comes from a basic misunderstanding about the acceptance tests. Remember that all the business rules are discussed during the specification workshops, so there should be at least one acceptance test covering every business rule that needs to be implemented. As the specification workshops help to build a shared understanding of the domain, the developers should also have a lot of tacit knowledge and a much better grasp of the domain without reading any additional documents.

With agile acceptance testing, the chosen set of acceptance tests represents the requirements. This is the authoritative source of information about the domain and the target system. It is kept alive and relevant throughout the project, so this is what the developers should be reading. You do not have to write a formal requirements document unless it helps you focus better, but if you do write one, keep it to yourself. If you are worried about features not being implemented because they are not in the acceptance tests, the best thing to do is to write some new new examples and tests.

What if I leave something out?

A common question I get during introductory workshops from business analysts is: 'what happens if something is not specified precisely in acceptance tests?' Realistic and precise examples leave no space for misinterpretation and they remove ambiguity from the specifications. The usual reason why features are left out is that the team is still learning how to implement acceptance testing and can't get everything done at first, or that there is a lack of information or insufficient access to domain experts when examples are being written.

The fear of these situations is caused by a misunderstanding that there is a moment when acceptance tests are handed over by the business analysts to developers and testers, in a similar way to formal requirements documents being signed off and passed down the pipeline. There is no such handover in agile acceptance testing. If anyone is to be the owner of acceptance tests, then this is the business analyst, and ownership stays with him.

The cost of change with agile development methods is relatively low compared to more traditional development processes. If your team is using an agile method, you can always add a new acceptance test later or change an existing test without causing much trouble. Just make sure that everyone else knows about the update. If you are making a large change try to discuss it during a workshop. Changes are a much bigger problem with a waterfall development process and this is probably why specification by example and agile acceptance testing had to wait for agile development methods to mature in order to gain momentum.

Although they will not openly admit this, some business analysts intentionally leave ambiguity in formal documents as a sort of a manoeuvering space for later. This allows them to change their mind or pass on the blame. Being able to pass on the blame is especially important in bureaucratic organisations, so ambiguity in requirements is actually a safety net for these people. I consider that using ambiguity as a safety net is a very bad and unfair practice that has no place in a good team. As the cost of later change is not large, there is no need for the safety net. This approach prepares for the failure of the project, not for success. If you as a business analyst, with a key role in a project, are preparing from the start for it to fail, what chance does it have of success?

In most cases, I find that the fear of blame is unfounded and that we can be much better off if everyone focuses on doing their job properly. If you work in an organisation that has a blame culture and you need to start covering your back even before the development starts, then you have much bigger organisational problems then those addressed by agile acceptance testing. If you recognise your own company in the previous sentence, instead of slacking and covering your back, it might be time to polish your resume. At least from what I've seen, there are plenty of much nicer places to work.

In addition, as agile acceptance testing involves developers and testers in the process of building the specification, the responsibility to make it correct and complete is shared. There is less pressure on the business analysts to get the requirements right on their own.

I won't understand user stories and tests, I'm used to use cases

User stories are not at all difficult to comprehend, and every single business analyst whom I've worked with and who has made a small effort to understand the underlying ideas got the picture very quickly. After all, it is not rocket science, it is just a different approach to the same problems that people have been dealing with for years. The issue is often not whether you will understand user stories and story tests, it is whether you *want* to understand them. Some people simply resist any change to the way they work and my only cure for this is to try and present the benefits as best as I can. This book is my attempt to do so on a large scale.

There is much excellent literature out there on user stories and I recommend starting with two books by Mike Cohn, *User Stories Explained*[11] and *Agile Estimating and Planning*[12]. Both are relatively short so you can read them on the bus or train on your way to work.

An important thing to remember is that user stories do not have to be perfect and it's not a problem if you don't get them right straight away. They are there primarily as a collaborative planning tool and to stimulate discussion. When you are using them, other people will be involved as well, helping you understand how to use them and to find better ways to exploit user stories. The situation with story tests is very similar. They still contain triggers, steps, exceptions and all the usual utilities in a business analyst's toolbox – they are just written down differently. Because tests are produced during the specification workshops, the other people will help you produce more complete tests and specifications. Developers will be there to help you write them down in the particular way required by your team's automation tool of choice.

It's impossible to describe non-functional requirements as tests

User interfaces, performance, usability and security requirements are very hard to describe effectively as automated acceptance tests. This is very often used as an argument against moving towards agile acceptance testing from a more traditional requirements and specification process. My counter-argument for this is that the biggest benefit of agile acceptance testing is in the conversation and building a shared understanding based around realistic examples. The fact that the user interface cannot be described as a FIT table or a BDD scenario does not prevent you from discussing the interface and providing examples during the specification workshop. Not everything can be automated, so what? You can find some ideas on how to deal with this issue in the section *What do we do with things that cannot be automated?* on page 90.

There is nothing preventing you from using a different tool or processes in addition to agile acceptance testing. The practice is not a magic wand that will make all your problems go away, but it will help you handle functional requirements much more effectively than with traditional processes. You can organise workshops with security experts and usability designers to help developers produce software that meets security and UI requirements. You can also schedule security probing, performance testing and usability reviews periodically every few weeks or months in addition to the functional test automation.

There is no big picture

Breaking business rules down into lots of realistic examples to illustrate all the variations in possibilities might make it hard to see the big picture. Business rules may become too scattered throughout the acceptance test sets and if you do not take care, they will become hard to understand after a while. However, most acceptance test tools allow you to group tests into hierarchies and add arbitrary descriptions to tests or groups of tests. Always group related examples together and provide descriptions of the relevant business rules to explain examples better. I've outlined some ideas on how to organise tests efficiently in the section *Organise tests so that they are easy to find* on page 134.

There is no traceability

When a single person acts as a gateway for all the requirements and everything is put into a single document, it is relatively easy to keep track of who ordered what and when, especially if the document is signed off before development starts. Because of the collaborative model of agile acceptance testing and because a single phase of development can be broken down into hundreds of small examples and tests, some people are concerned about the traceability of requirements and specifications. After all, implementing a requirement costs money and someone ultimately has to approve and pay for it.

I don't like sign-offs and prefer to work closely with the customers on building the system that they need. However, if you need to get official approval, treat the formal set of acceptance tests as the specification and get a sign-off on it. Most test automation and management tools allow you to put arbitrary comments on tests, so you can include the name of the person who approved a particular test and the date when it was approved. If you implement strict ownership, which anyway I think is a bad idea, you can list the name of the person who owns a particular test as well.

When user stories are used for project planning, acceptance tests are derived from stories and you can implement traceability by linking individual tests to a story, then linking stories to customer benefits and project goals. You can track who requested a story and when on individual story cards, or you can put this information into an acceptance test hierarchy.

If the tests are stored in a version control system, as I recommend in the section *Keep tests in a version control system* on page 135, then it is also very easy to go back and inspect who changed a test, when and why. Most source version control systems give you this functionality out of the box.

 ## Stuff to remember

- The role of the business analyst is changing from that of a conveyor of information to that of a facilitator who enables people to share knowledge directly.
- The business analyst is a great choice for the facilitator of the specification workshop.
- Working with acceptance tests makes the rest of the business analyst's work easier and more effective.
- You can still keep your traditional documents, but use acceptance tests as the authoritative specification.
- You can modify the specification (acceptance tests) when the development starts without causing great problems for anyone.
- There should be no handover of tests from business analysts to developers or testers.
- Tests don't have to be perfect from the start.
- Getting it right is not your sole responsibility. Developers and testers share responsibility for the specifications.

Chapter 13
Effects on testers

In 2005 I worked with a development organisation that had a remote testing department. The testing team was considered completely ineffective since many problems passed undetected through them, and developers generally considered talking to the testing department as a waste of time. To be fair to the testers, they were expected to grasp instantly whatever the developers produced and test it without knowing the first thing about it. Nobody wanted to spend any time explaining anything to them and there was simply no feedback in the whole process. I think that having a detached testing team simply does not work, nor does getting testers involved at the end. In the words of Philip Crosby, "Quality has to be caused, not controlled". This does not mean that there is no place for testers in agile processes – far from it – but that the role of the tester has to change. Agile acceptance testing is a great manifestation of this.

The new role of the tester

Mary Poppendieck talked about her experiences of moving to a lean production process at Google Tech Talks on the 15th of December 2006, in a session titled *Competing on the Basis of Speed*.[1] Although her experiences relate to manufacturing, I think that they perfectly describe what the role of the tester in software development should be and why this is important. She said:

> *When we started up in our plant, we had people in QA who used to try to find defects in our products, and we moved them all out on to the production line to figure out how to make stuff without defects in the first place...You will be amazed at how much faster you go when you make stuff and defects are caught when they occur instead of being found later.*

---

[1]http://video.google.com/videoplay?docid=-5105910452864283694

Instead of acting as controllers at the end of the project, testers should help developers and business analysts avoid problems. Agile acceptance testing allows testers to suggest how a piece of software should be verified, rather than manually test the software themselves. Testers need to communicate concerns and possible pitfalls from the testing perspective during specification workshops and warn business people and developers about important edge cases that they have missed.

By taking an active participation in the specification workshops, testers learn about the domain and the expected system behaviour first hand. This solves the problem of testers not really knowing anything about the system when the time comes to approve a release. The knowledge gained during the workshop will be instrumental in writing, expanding and refining tests.

Benefits for testers

As a quick recap of Part II, let's go back to the benefits promised in the introduction and see how the practices of agile acceptance testing deliver them.

You can stop developers from making the same mistakes over and over

If you've had some experience working with the development team, you surely know what kind of mistakes they are likely to make. Instead of checking manually for the same problems over and over again and returning the release back to the developers because of these issues, you can prevent the problems from happening in the first place. The specification workshops allow you to suggest these typical problems as examples that should be discussed and put into the acceptance test suite. Discussing the examples with developers helps them learn and helps prevent similar mistakes in the future. Including tests for typical problems in the acceptance test suite ensures that developers sort out these issues before submitting the system for testing in the first place.

As you can add tests for any bugs found in production to the acceptance test suite, you can be sure that the bugs will not resurface, or at least that the developers will find out about resurrected bugs and fix them before you need to get involved.

You will have a much better understanding of the domain

If you participate in the specification workshops and learn about the goals of iterations you will understand the system at a much deeper level than if you had simply read specifications after development. Even better, the process of building a shared understanding during the workshop ensures that your ideas about the system are consistent with what the customers want and what other members of the implementation team understand.

You'll delegate a lot of dull work to developers

Agile acceptance testing relies heavily on the automation of tests and you will benefit from this. There will be a solid foundation for the automation of most of the QA process, so that you do not have to perform tests manually. Even better, instead of you automating the tests on your own, this responsibility is either given completely to developers or shared with them. Your job is to participate in proposing the tests that should be automated. So you save a lot of time because you won't have to run tests manually or spend time automating them. You will have much more time for verifying things that cannot be automated easily and other important tasks.

You can build in quality from the start

Instead of having a reactive role, trying to catch problems in a developed system, agile acceptance testing puts you in the driving seat and allows you to avoid problems. You can build quality into the software from the start by suggesting examples that would break or cheat the system during the specification workshops. The ensuing discussion will help you to teach developers how to think more like you and what they need to do to make the product better.

You'll be able to verify business rules at the touch of a button

Agile acceptance testing incrementally produces a set of regression tests as the software is being implemented. This set of tests is automated and you can execute it at the touch of a button, allowing you to verify and reverify the business rules implemented in the system.

Because developers automate tests to connect directly to business code, not through the user interface, tests run much more quickly than if you automated them using one of the classic UI test robots. I don't mean to say that having automated UI tests using robots is bad, by all means use them when it makes sense. But you don't have to verify business rules with such tests – automated acceptance tests provide a much more efficient way to do this.

You will have a lot more time for experimenting

Because automated acceptance tests already give you a level of confidence in business rules, you will have a lot more time for experimenting with the system. Because you are involved in writing examples, building the specification and creating acceptance tests, you will have a much better understanding of which areas have not been considered or covered in enough detail, so that you can focus your exploratory testing effort more accurately.

This is one of the key contributions that testers should make to the project. Developers and business analysts think about the system from the perspective of making it work and they usually don't try to use the system in unexpected ways or go down unpredictable paths.

Testers, on the other hand, are specialised in this. By giving you more time to do this, agile acceptance testing empowers you to perform better exploratory testing and provide much better feedback from your experiments.

Having more time for experimenting also allows you to refine and expand the suite of regression tests based on what you learn during exploratory testing and to suggest more possible problems in workshops for iterations to come. So acceptance testing, test automation and exploratory testing are linked together in a positive reinforcing loop.

Better relationships in the team

Agile acceptance testing also helps to build better teams and bring people together. When the primary role of testers is to find defects, they are often seen as adversaries of developers. Developers and testers can consider each other as rivals. With agile acceptance testing, nobody has to be a bad guy. The specification workshops require people of different profiles to work together and helps testers build in quality from the start without getting into conflict with developers. From my experience, I can state emphatically that bringing people together to discuss the examples during the workshops also helps to build trust, mutual respect and personal understanding among the participants, transforming disparate groups of individuals into teams.

By working closely together with developers, you will learn more about the system architecture and implementation and you will be able to provide better feedback. Developers will start to respect your input much more than if you were working separately. As testers are required to participate during the specification workshops, your opinions will matter and business people will notice this and listen to you.

Challenges for testers

Here are some of the questions and concerns about agile acceptance testing I hear from testers during my talks, workshops and tutorials.

I don't want to lose control over testing

Testing managers, especially those in big corporate organisations, often look at agile acceptance testing as another attempt by developers to take over part of their territory and resist this change with all the power they have. In my view, this is plain silly and always has to do much more with corporate politics than reality. If anything, agile acceptance testing gives testers more responsibility and control. It doesn't stop you doing any kind of verification that you were planning to do, but it does transfer much of the more boring manual testing onto the shoulders of developers, who then automate most or all of it. So you are not giving away control over testing, you are obtaining tools to do it more efficiently and involving more people in testing.

Agile acceptance testing gives testers much more influence over the project – the testing department can finally have a say in what gets produced, not just what gets fixed. It also allows you to be more productive in testing, because you will run into fewer blocking issues as key concerns will have been communicated before development starts.

It's cheating

A very strange argument I have heard on a few occasions against agile acceptance testing is that it is effectively cheating. The argument goes that with agile acceptance testing, testers are required to tell the developers exactly what they are going to check, so the developers can implement the software to pass the tests upfront.

I honestly struggle to understand why this is a problem. Software development, at least in my eyes, is a cooperative activity and not a competition. If the developers don't put the problem into the system in the first place, it's more efficient than you catching the problem later and returning it back to them for fixing. It does not matter who put the bug in, who caught it and who fixed it. Agile acceptance testing asks us to not create the bug in the first place.

Unfortunately, agile acceptance testing has no chance of success in companies where people earn money on metrics such as bugs found and bugs resolved. If your salary or bonus depend on such statistics, you are not going to like agile acceptance testing one bit. On the other hand, if you consider improving the quality of the software as your job, not catching bugs, then this practice can help you greatly to do it more efficiently.

The idea of giving developers tests upfront is similar to the idea of publicising where speed cameras are on the motorway. The goal of introducing speed cameras is to reduce accidents, not to charge people for speeding. If you tell everyone where the cameras are and if there are enough cameras on the most accident-prone parts of the road system, people almost always stop speeding there. Testers on an agile team should ensure that there are enough speed cameras and that they are placed on all parts of the road that are likely to cause accidents.

Will I lose my job because of this automation?

Some testers whom I've spoken to about this practice fear that they will be made redundant by test automation. Test automation, for things that can be automated, is coming regardless of agile acceptance testing. It is going to happen whether testers are on board or not. I really think that the days of manual testing scripts written down on paper and carefully executed by twenty testers over two weeks are numbered. This kind of testing will never be completely rooted out, just as there are still jobs for COBOL programmers, but most testing activity in the future will not revolve around manual execution of test scripts.

A very important thing to realise is that test automation does not replace human testers, it helps them do their work better and leaves more time for things that require human intelligence and touch. This includes manual exploratory testing, looking for inconsistencies, testing with more extreme conditions, performance, security and usability testing. Instead of swimming against the current, use the change to your advantage. Partial automation even helps testers to do exploratory testing better, by by speeding up the boring parts.

I would argue that, rather than endangering testers' jobs, agile acceptance testing increases their importance to the company and make their jobs more secure. It offers several options for career advancement, including becoming an automation specialist or a domain specialist.

A tester with domain knowledge is absolutely irreplaceable, even with a totally agile development process and aggressive test automation. I learned this the hard way, while working on a new trading application for a big online betting system. We did everything by the book, had good customer involvement, business analysts who participated in the project and a development process that could be considered agile by most standards. Because testing was outsourced and ineffi- cient, we decided to ignore the testing department and rely on auto- mated tests that we did ourselves, although we still had to hand over the system for formal testing eventually. The outsourced testing department never found anything really serious. I later realised that this was because they had no idea what they were testing. No-one was interested in sharing domain knowledge. Before the first release, the company hired a senior tester from one of their clients. This woman had worked on similar systems for a long time and knew the business domain inside and out. Coming from a QA perspective, she had excellent ideas about how to break the system and knew exactly where it might be vulnerable. We agreed to let her have a go at our system just for fun, confident that automated unit and acceptance tests protected us from problems. It was a very painful experience to watch her tear the application apart. She did not find any serious problems in business rules, but she found loads of small embarrassing issues in the first ten minutes of smoke testing. I learned to respect the skills and experience of testers as very important additions to the skills and insights of developers and business people.

I believe that testers have a completely different view of software systems than developers or business analysts. They think about breaking and cheating the system, in addition to verifying that it works. Although developers are typically good at identifying edge cases in business rules, they rarely check the user interface properly and they don't approach the system with the intention of breaking it. This is exactly why testers need to participate in the specification workshops and point out these cases. Developers and business analysts are often simply blind when it comes to this.

If you are worried about your job, learn all you can about the business domain. With a testing mind-set and business knowledge, you can help developers and business people see their blind spots. This will make your contribution much more visible and your position much more important. Specification workshops help you do this because you will be right there with the experts, getting the chance to learn about the domain and discuss the software before it gets developed.

Mike Scott wrote[2] that he had noticed the blending of analyst and tester roles: "when we start recognising the tests as executable specifications you rapidly realise that the role is practically the same". He gives the example of a client organisation that makes no distinction between testers and business analysts, and just has a single analyst role. According to Scott the only problems with this are personal, as business analysts tend to think of a test role as a demotion. I noticed the same thing in an organisation that I provided consultancy to in early 2008, where one of the business analysts was really enthusiastic about acceptance testing but her superior rejected the idea. The analyst was given permission to participate in acceptance testing provided her role was renamed to test analyst. Her boss insisted that she was no longer a business analyst if she was involved in anything related to testing.

---

[2]in a private e-mail

Antony Marcano suggested a career path for testers who have an inclination for programming and developers who demonstrate an aptitude for testing, during his talk on *Understanding QA/Testing on Agile Projects*[3] in September 2008 in London. By growing their skills in these areas, they may become what Marcano calls tester-developers or developer-testers. Microsoft is also promoting this idea,[4] calling this role *software design engineer in test* (SDET). An SDET has the following responsibilities: testing software components and interfaces in more technical depth, writing test programs to assure quality and developing test tools to increase effectiveness. Marcano thinks[5] that this will soon become the norm for testers and developers alike and draws a parallel between developer-testers and the blending of analyst and programmer roles in earlier times. The role of analyst-programmer was introduced because developers were increasingly expected to perform systems analysis. Analysis was then taken as one of the responsibilities of programmers and the analyst-programmer title was later simplified to just developer.

Another very interesting career option is to become an automation specialist and learn how to bridge the gap between examples coming out of the workshop and domain code. In general, automation specialists are paid more than click-testers and there seems to be a healthy demand for people that know their way around Fitnesse, Selenium and similar tools at the moment. This career path might be especially interesting for technical people who know a bit about programming and possibly came to QA from a programming background. Automating tests requires some basic programming skills, but it does not demand that you know all about the latest frameworks and technologies.

In any case, agile acceptance testing practices can help you on this path as well, as it encourages you to work closely with developers. Pair up with a developer and learn how they write fixtures and automate tests, then start taking over these parts of the role.

---

[3]http://skillsmatter.com/podcast/home/understanding-qatesting-on-agile-projects
[4]http://members.microsoft.com/careers/careerpath/technical/softwaretesting.mspx
[5]http://www.testingreflections.com/node/view/7280

Acceptance tests will not catch all problems

Agile acceptance testing is not a silver bullet and it would be silly to expect that it will magically catch all problems. Again, the focus of the practice is much more on building a shared understanding of the domain and guiding the development then on quality control.

Some things cannot be easily automated and every tool that you decide to use will have its good and bad sides. But applying agile acceptance testing does not prevent you from running any other tests or using different tools. It even gives you more time to focus on things that cannot be caught by acceptance tests. Instead of verifying every single business rule, you can be confident that they are correct and spend more time sanity testing or running exploratory tests.

User interface validations are not likely to be fully automated in the immediate future. This is where testers will still need to utilise their skills. But instead of verifying business rules, which should be covered by acceptance tests, you can just focus on checking that the actual user interface is solid and that it works as expected.

Also, while a team is learning how to use agile acceptance testing and getting buy-in from their business users or customers, it is likely that some things will still fall though the communication gap. Instead of using this to point out flaws in agile acceptance testing, I urge you to work out why things were missed in the first place and help improve the specification workshop for the next iteration. As a tester, your job is to come up with bug prevention strategies, not to find bugs at the end.

 Stuff to remember

- The new primary role of testers is to help people avoid problems, not to discover them.

- The QA process does not end with agile acceptance testing. You can still use any other tool or technique in addition to acceptance tests.
- The automation of acceptance tests gives you more time to test things that cannot be easily automated, where human intelligence and touch are important.
- Testers have more clout in projects that use agile acceptance testing.
- Develop your career by learning all you can about the domain during specification workshops, or become an automation specialist.

Chapter 14
Effects on developers

Although the role of developers changes with the introduction of agile acceptance testing, I find that they are generally enthusiastic about the idea and do not put up any resistance. From a technical perspective, most developers see it just as an extension of test-driven development principles, and TDD is now becoming well established among software developers. However developers are sometimes overly enthusiastic and forget about the requirement to collaborate. They take over more responsibility than they should, losing the benefits of shared understanding and communication.

New responsibilities for developers

Agile acceptance testing requires developers to take a more active part in the process of eliciting requirements and building a specification of what is to be developed. Many senior developers already do this, especially on agile teams, so this is just a reinforcement of the requirement. If your team leaves the creation of specifications entirely to business analysts and customers, then it is time to get more involved.

A major change introduced by agile acceptance testing is the requirement for developers to participate in domain discussions, evolving their own understanding of the domain and providing much needed technical expertise during the specification workshops. Although this duty has nothing to do with writing code, you should take it very seriously as it will help you write the code much more effectively later. While the examples are being worked out, it is the role of developers to think ahead about implementation challenges, identifying functional gaps and technical edge cases, suggesting them for discussion and explaining to business people why these cases matter. Business people often have a very focused perspective of the system, concentrating on how it should behave when it works correctly and ignoring things they consider minor problems. These same problems could be really significant for developers, because it is their necks that are on the line when something does not work. A former colleague of mine whined about the fact that the business people he worked for refused to discuss a potential problem because the chances of it happening were only one in a million. From the perspective of the business people, the problem was irrelevant. On the other hand, the system they were supporting processed about 200,000 business transactions a day, so for my colleague 'one in a million' meant that he would be called in at least once a week to troubleshoot serious data consistency problems. Developers need to raise awareness about such concerns and get them properly discussed and resolved during specification workshops.

Benefits for developers

As a quick recap of Part II, let's go back to the promises made in the introduction and see how agile acceptance testing makes them come true.

Functional gaps will be flushed out before development

With the focus on realistic examples and writing them down as formal acceptance tests, it is easy to spot inconsistencies and gaps in the requirements during specification workshops. Writing down examples has the same effect as writing code, making it obvious when a particular case is not covered. While the examples are being discussed and written down, developers should try to think about implementation challenges and possible edge cases that also need to be discussed. Once the gaps and edge cases are identified, they should be discussed and resolved while the business people are in the room and focused on the problem. Using this process, we collaboratively produce a development specification that is much more detailed, complete and consistent than traditional requirements specifications. Gaps should no longer be identified only once we start developing code, when the business people might no longer be readily available to discuss them.

Business analysts will really understand special cases

If you are unclear about a particular example or if you suspect that there is an important edge case that needs to be covered, you can offer it for discussion during a specification workshop. If business people seem unconcerned with the example, explain first why it is important and what difference it makes. Examples based on precise realistic information require people to think harder and offer precise results, so they will not be able to just brush the question off. Go through the example and work out together whether it is important enough to be added to the specification. The primary goal of the specification workshop is to build a shared understanding of the domain, so a discussion on an edge case should end either by everyone agreeing that the example is not important and knowing why it is not important, or everyone agreeing that it is important and working out how the system should behave in this case.

Automated tests will be your targets for development

Acceptance tests provide us with a universally agreed target for development. They should cover all important cases (or at least most of them) so that we can focus on implementing only what is specified in these cases. Examples that were not selected for the set of acceptance tests are not relevant for the project or not important for the current phase of development, so we do not have to think about implementing code just in case.

Because tests are automated, it is easy to check whether the code implements the specification correctly and completely. A failing test suggests that we need to implement additional functionality. When all the tests pass, we know that the work is done. If a previously passing test fails, we have broken something.

Code will be easier to share, hand over and take over

An acceptance test serves not only as a specification of what the code should do before it is developed, but also as a description of what the code does after implementation. Because tests are executable and kept in synchronisation with the code, this description is accurate and authoritative. Acceptance tests are much more concise than code, so they are a lot easier to read and understand.

Having a set of acceptance tests to describe what a code module does makes it much easier to share it with someone else. They will not have to read through the code or depend on you to describe it. The first thing I do typically when new members join my team is to give them a brief introduction to the project and then let them read existing acceptance tests to get to know the system better.

Having this kind of live documentation is also very useful when you need to hand over the code to another team or organisation.

Challenges for developers

Here are some of the questions and concerns about agile acceptance testing I hear from developers during my talks, workshops and tutorials.

I don't have time to write fixtures or maintain tests

Technically, agile acceptance testing introduces new work for developers, but not necessarily more work. By new work I mean that developers have to participate in writing tests, write the automation code and maintain it. On the other hand, this should produce a much more accurate and clear target for development, reducing later rework caused by misunderstandings or incomplete specifications. From my experience, the overall result is much less work for developers rather then more work, although in the beginning this new work does seem to be additional.

One potential issue with this is that the benefits of agile acceptance testing are not that obvious or instant. You won't necessarily notice straightaway that you have less rework to do, since there is usually a time lag between delivery of code and requests for rework arriving. The reductions in bug numbers and change requests are also hard to spot when you are looking only at the current iteration. To truly evaluate the benefits of agile acceptance testing, you have to look at the way you work from a wider perspective and compare the whole process after the introduction of acceptance testing with the way it was before.

Acceptance tests turn out to be incomplete

Ideally, we want to flush out all edge cases and discover all functional gaps in the specification workshops, and agile acceptance testing normally helps greatly in this direction. However, sometimes things slip through the net, especially when you are just starting to use agile acceptance testing. If you start developing code and run into an unidentified case, grab a business analyst or customer representative and discuss it. Don't just go ahead and assume that you know how the system should work. You should also discuss why the case was missed during the workshop and whether any other rules are affected by it. When you discuss the case, take care not to over-generalise and go beyond the scope of the current iteration. Things that were intentionally left out of scope should not creep back into the system.

The discovery of many new edge cases in development is typically a signal that the specification workshop didn't function properly or didn't take place at all. The workshop should not be a one-way event where the customer or a business analyst presents his ideas and developers who then go away and implement them. A workshop like this will have the same consequences as the orders of battalion commanders as described in the section *Imperative requirements are very easy to misunderstand* on page 8. An effective workshop requires the active participation of all participants. Only then can we build a shared understanding of the domain.

Participating in the specification workshops is not a waste of time, it is the best chance to learn about the domain and the right time to identify and discuss functional gaps. It should be considered as one of the key responsibilities of programmers, not as something unimportant that can be done on a voluntary basis.

Can't we just write the tests ourselves?

Developers often see acceptance tests more as larger unit tests then as a communication technique, and therein lies one of the biggest pitfalls of agile acceptance testing.

While writing unit tests before code is recommended, sometimes writing code and unit tests in parallel works fine as well. If I am unsure about a particular case after I have written the code, I can quickly write a unit test to verify it. This does not work for acceptance tests, or at least not in the same way. With unit tests, developers own the code and they should perfectly understand how it is intended to work. This is why writing a unit test in parallel with the code is not a problem. However, acceptance tests must always be written before the code, because they specify what the system should do. By adding an acceptance test, you are extending the specification of the system and making a business decision about the domain. You are then effectively taking on the role of the customer.

Any additional tests or changes to existing tests must be discussed with business people, just in case there is a mismatch in what you think it should do and what they think it should do. As you gain more knowledge about the domain, you will make better and better guesses, but no guess should go unverified.

The worst thing developers can do is to write acceptance tests on their own just to have good code coverage or to tick a box that the project has acceptance tests. Writing acceptance tests after the code just to pass a test-coverage criterion is pointless, because you are writing a specification based on what was already developed. The only exception to this that I can think of is where you build a set of tests to document what a legacy system does before it is improved or modified.

Rather than waiting for a phase of the project to end and then discovering parts of the code that are not covered by tests, chase your business people to help you with defining how the system should behave before developing these parts. Once you have some experience, you will identify most of these cases in the specification workshop anyway, so you should not have such a big problem with code test coverage.

If there is no buy-in from the business side and they do not want to discuss examples, I would suggest that you are better off without the acceptance tests than with acceptance tests that you make up yourselves. At least you will not have a misleading specification.

This does not mean that developers cannot write functional tests at all. Unit tests, component tests and integration tests can and should all be written to reflect the developer's view of the system and concerns with a particular piece of code or way of working. They might even be automated using the same tools as acceptance tests, but they are not a replacement for them, and neither do they in any way make up for the communication benefits obtained through specification workshops.

There is too much duplication

With acceptance tests and unit tests in place, developers often notice duplication, which they typically don't like. Duplication in code is one thing, and we are right to fight against it relentlessly, but duplication in tests is something else and is not such a bad thing. Unit tests and acceptance tests serve completely different purposes. Unit tests verify technical correctness from the developer's perspective.

Acceptance tests verify functional correctness from the customer's perspective. The same piece of code can be subjected to both verifications separately. Having said this, once acceptance tests come into play, you can really focus unit tests only on technical correctness and not write any business rule unit tests. This takes some time to get used to, but it is a good way to remove some of the duplication. See the section *Unit tests vs acceptance tests* on page 113 for an example.

Acceptance tests are written based on examples developed during the specification workshops, so there will often be some duplication even in the examples or tests themselves. Again, this is not necessarily a bad thing. If the system is easier to comprehend and explain with a bit of duplication, leave it in. On the other hand, duplication in specifications and acceptance tests might also suggest that we are missing an important abstraction that should be made explicit to make the system easier to understand.

Some acceptance test automation tools allow you to extract common parts of tests into a shared set-up or separate components that can be included in other tests. As a developer, it is your job to suggest such changes so that tests become easier to maintain.

Resist the urge to restructure and reorganise tests so that they are easy to maintain but no longer easy to understand. Acceptance tests are not code. They need to be used for communication with business people over the life of the project, so they have to be able to read and understand them. If you reformat a test so that only a developer can understand it, you might as well throw it away.

I cannot run acceptance tests from my IDE

Agile acceptance testing tools are designed for collaboration rather than for efficient development, for business users rather than for developers. Comparing acceptance tests to unit tests again, this situation makes life more difficult for developers. Most integrated development environments now allow you to run unit tests directly from the code-editing window, shortening the loop between developing and verifying a piece of code. Acceptance tests cover much larger parts of the code, so it is not so easy to work out exactly what they relate to, and current tools often lack good IDE integration. One of the biggest complaints is that it is often much harder to debug code under acceptance tests than with a unit test. The biggest benefit of agile acceptance testing is improved communication and collaboration. This easily outweighs the importance of close integration and easy debugging during test runs.

The only thing I can offer as a consolation is that tools are evolving. One of the most important areas where tools need to improve is to provide multiple views for different people, so that developers can keep working from an IDE and business people can use something more convenient for them. For the time being, tools are a big problem for everyone, but the point of agile acceptance testing is not in tools but in the conversation.

Unit tests give us better feedback

Acceptance tests are often compared to unit tests by developers, although they do not solve the same problems. Acceptance tests deal with larger pieces of code and longer development efforts, so you don't get the satisfaction of instant feedback provided by unit tests. Slower feedback and the pain of maintaining the glue between acceptance test descriptions and domain code can cause disappointment among developers with acceptance testing, because they do not see any quick benefits. A common complaint from developers is that unit tests give them much better and faster feedback on the code.

You need to understand that acceptance tests are not really there to provide feedback on the code, so expecting them to do so is a mistake. Acceptance tests are primarily a communication tool for people. Comparing them to unit tests, even from a developer perspective, does not make any sense. Use normal unit tests to drive the development of small pieces of code, use acceptance tests to guide the overall effort.

Stuff to remember

- You cannot write acceptance tests yourself.
- You need to participate in domain discussions.
- Specification workshops give you a good chance to discuss edge cases and inconsistencies with domain experts before development.
- Acceptance tests do not provide instant feedback as unit tests do. This is because they deal with the overall picture and business rules, not code units.
- You need both unit tests and acceptance tests.
- Acceptance tests exist to facilitate communication between people.

Appendix A.
Resources

Books and articles

[1] Tracy Reppert. Copyright © 2004. Software Quality Engineering. *Better Software Magazine: Don't just break software, make software.* July/August 2004.

[2] Frederick P. Brooks. Copyright © 1995. Addison-Wesley Professional. *The Mythical Man-Month: Essays on Software Engineering, Anniversary Edition (2nd Edition).* 0201835959.

[3] Gerald M. Weinberg and Donald C. Gause. Copyright © 1989. Dorset House Publishing Company. *Exploring Requirements: Quality Before Design.* 0932633137.

[4] Gary Klein. Copyright © 1999. The MIT Press. *Sources of Power: How People Make Decisions.* 0262611465.

[5] Bertrand Russell. Copyright © 1985. Open Court Publishing Company. *The Philosophy of Logical Atomism.* 0875484433.

[6] James Surowiecki. Copyright © 2005. Addison-Wesley Professional. *The Wisdom of Crowds.* 0385721706.

[7] Tom Davenport. Copyright © 2003. CXO Media Inc. *CIO Magazine: A Measurable Proposal.* June 2003.

[8] Robert C. Martin and Grigori Melnik. Copyright © 2008. *IEEE Software: Tests and Requirements, Requirements and Tests: a Mobius Strip.* January/February 2008. page 54.

[9] Rick Mugridge and Ward Cunningham. Copyright © 2005. Prentice Hall PTR. *Fit for Developing Software: Framework for Integrated Tests.* 978-0321269348.

[10] David Lorge Parnas, Ryszard Janicki, and Jeffery Zucker. Copyright © 1996. Springer Verlag. *Relational Methods in Computer Science:Tabular representations in relational documents* . pages 184-196. 978-3-211-82971-4.

[11] Mike Cohn. Copyright © 2004. Addison-Wesley Professional. *User Stories Applied: For Agile Software Development.* 978-0321205681.

[12] Mike Cohn. Copyright © 2005. Prentice Hall PTR. *Agile Estimating and Planning (Robert C. Martin Series).* 0131479415.

[13] Eric Evans. Copyright © 2003. Addison-Wesley Professional. *Domain-Driven Design: Tackling Complexity in the Heart of Software.* 0321125215.

[14] Karl Weick. Copyright © 1984. Jossey-Bass. *The Executive Mind: Managerial thought in the context of action.* 0875895840. pages 221-242.

[15] Shigeo Shingo. Copyright © 1986. Productivity Press. *Zero Quality Control: Source Inspection and the Poka-Yoke System.* 0915299070.

[16] Mary Poppendieck and Tom Poppendieck. Copyright © 2003. Addison-Wesley Professional. *Lean Software Development: An Agile Toolkit.* 0321150783.

[17] George L. Kelling and James Q. Wilson. Copyright © 1982. The Atlantic Monthly Group. *Atlantic Monthly: Broken Windows.* March 1982.

[18] Andrew Hunt. David Thomas. Copyright © 1999. Addison-Wesley Professional. *Pragmatic Programmer: From Journeyman to Master.* 978-0201616224.

[19] Ellen Gottesdiener. Copyright © 2002. Addison-Wesley Professional. *Requirements by Collaboration: Workshops for Defining Needs.* 0201786060.

[20] Steve McConnell. Copyright © 2000. *IEEE Software: Cargo Cult Software Engineering.* March/April 2000.

[21] Mary Poppendieck and Tom Poppendieck. Copyright © 2006. Addison-Wesley Publishing Company. *Implementing Lean Software Development: From Concept to Cash.* 0321437381.

[22] Gojko Adzic. Copyright © 2008. Neuri Limited. *Test Driven .NET Development With FitNesse.* 0955683602.

[23] Jennitta Andrea. Copyright © 2007. *IEEE Software: Envisioning the Next Generation of Functional Testing Tools.* May/June 2007.

Online resources

Here are the links to all the online resources mentioned in the book. You can find all these links and more on the accompanying web site http://www.acceptancetesting.info.

Talks and videos

- Adam Geras: *Virtual Machines to support testing* from Agile 2008. http://video.google.com/videoplay?docid=-6298610650460170080
- Antony Marcano: *Understanding QA/Testing on Agile Projects* from Skills Matter Agile Month in 2008. http://skillsmatter.com/podcast/home/understanding-qatesting-on-agile-projects
- Elisabeth Hendrickson: *Things that change* from Agile 2008. http://video.google.com/videoplay?docid=8565239121902737883
- Gojko Adzic: *Introduction to Agile Acceptance Testing* from Skills Matter Agile Month in 2008. http://gojko.net/2008/09/19/agile-acceptance-testing-video/
- Martin Fowler and Dan North *The Yawning Crevasse of Doom* from QCon London 2007. http://www.infoq.com/presentations/Fowler-North-Crevasse-of-Doom

- Mary Poppendieck: *Competing on the basis of speed* from Google Tech Talks in 2006. http://video.google.com/videoplay?docid=-5105910452864283694
- Rick Mugridge: *Doubling the value of automated tests* from Google Tech Talks in London in 2006. http://video.google.co.uk/videoplay?docid=-7227306990557696708

Presentations

- Gilles Mantel: *Test Driven Requirements Workshop* from Agile 2008. http://testdriveninformation.blogspot.com/2008/08/material-of-tdr-workshop-at-agile-2008.html
- Michael Phoenix: *Domain Specific Testing Languages* from Agile 2008. http://www.solutionsiq.com/agile2008/agile-2008-domain.php
- Naresh Jain: *Acceptance Test Driven Development.* http://www.slideshare.net/nashjain/acceptance-test-driven-development-350264

Articles

- Brian Marick: *An Alternative to Business-Facing TDD.* http://www.exampler.com/blog/2008/03/23/an-alternative-to-business-facing-tdd/
- Brian Marick: *My Agile testing project.* http://www.exampler.com/old-blog/2003/08/21/
- Dan North: *Introducing BDD.* http://dannorth.net/introducing-bdd
- Gojko Adzic: *Fitting Agile Acceptance Testing into the development process.* http://gojko.net/2008/09/17/fitting-agile-acceptance-testing-into-the-development-process/
- Jennitta Andrea: *Envisioning the next generation of functional testing tools.* http://www.jennittaandrea.com/wp-content/uploads/2007/04/envisioningthenextgenerationoffunctionaltestingtools_ieeesw_may2007.pdf

- Jim Shore: *How I Use Fit*. http://jamesshore.com/Blog/How-I-Use-Fit.html
- Robert C. Martin and Grigori Melnik: *Tests and Requirements, Requirements and Tests: A Mobius Strip*. http://www.gmelnik.com/papers/IEEE_Software_Moebius_GMelnik_RMartin.pdf
- Ron Jeffries: *Essential XP: Card, Conversation, Confirmation*. http://www.xprogramming.com/xpmag/expCardConversationConfirmation.htm
- Tracy Reppert: *Don't just break software, make software*. http://industriallogic.com/papers/storytest.pdf

Tools

- Concordion: http://www.concordion.org
- Cubic Test: http://www.cubictest.com
- FitNesse main web site: http://fitnesse.org
- FitNesse community site: http://www.fitnesse.info
- Green Pepper: http://www.greenpeppersoftware.com/en/products/
- JBehave: http://jbehave.org
- JUseCase: http://jusecase.sourceforge.net/
- PyUseCase: http://sourceforge.net/projects/pyusecase
- Selenium: http://selenium.openqa.org/
- StoryTestIQ: http://storytestiq.solutionsiq.com
- Twist: http://studios.thoughtworks.com/twist-agile-test-automation/
- Text Test: http://www.texttest.org

Mailing Lists

- Agile acceptance testing (the companion mailing list to this book): http://groups.google.com/group/agileacceptancetesting
- Agile Testing: http://tech.groups.yahoo.com/group/agile-testing

- Agile Alliance Functional Testing Tools: http://tech.groups.yahoo.com/group/aa-ftt/
- Concordion: http://tech.groups.yahoo.com/group/concordion/
- FitNesse: http://tech.groups.yahoo.com/group/fitnesse/

Index

Symbols

.NET tools 176

A

The story continues online

You can find more about agile acceptance testing and specification by example on the companion web site http://www.acceptancetesting.info, where you can also register your copy of the book to get free PDF updates.

Sign up to the Agile Acceptance Testing mailing list on Google Groups (http://groups.google.com/group/agileacceptancetesting) to discuss this book with other readers.

For more from the same author, see http://gojko.net.